MW00861183

Quantum Leap:

How to Make a
Quantum Leap in Your
Network Marketing Business

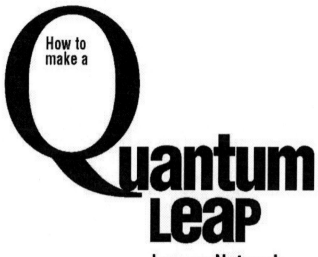

How to make a Quantum Leap

In your Network Marketing Business

by **Toni Coleman Brown**

Quantum Leap
Productions, LLC
GOING TO ANOTHER LEVEL

Far Rockaway, NY
www.qlproductions.com

Published by
Quantum Leap Productions, LLC.
444 Beach 22nd Street, Far Rockaway, NY 11691
www.qlproductions.com

International Standard Book Number: 0-9787568-0-0
Library of Congress Catalog Card Number: 2006930511

Copy Edited by Diane Falvey
Content Edited by Monica Harris
Cover Designed by Maria Ackies of GinaMarie Designs

Acknowledgements

This book has been a true labor of love. It is my hope that it has the power to help anyone who picks it up and follows the key strategies. I would like to thank the many people who have helped me create this project:

First and foremost, I would like to thank my family: my husband, Sandy, and my daughters, Taylor and Sasha, who allow me to be who I am.

I would also like to thank the members of the Xtreme Dream Team, where "Everything Is Possible." I want you to know that each of you helped to make this possible.

Thank you to my mom, Antoinette T. Coleman, for being such an inspiration and for truly believing in me. And Daddy, may you rest in peace knowing that your baby girl is living her dreams. We miss you. To my brothers and sisters, Lee Coleman, Melvin Coleman, Dorelia Harrison, and Elvina Coleman, know that each of you have played a part in shaping my life.

And special thanks to my contributors, C. Thomas Gambrell, Tracey Hughes, Alvin Day, Niambi Jarvis, and Barbara Page.

To my editors, Diane Falvey and Monica Harris, you ladies are the best. Maria Ackies you are the best Art Director in the world.

A special thank you goes to everyone at Warm Spirit, especially Nadine, Daniel, and the entire S.O.S. Team.

TABLE OF CONTENTS

Part I

Part II

Part III

Preface

My name is Toni Coleman Brown. I grew up in a two-parent home in New Orleans, Louisiana, where neither of my parents graduated from high school. What they lacked in formal education however, they more than made up for in life experience. I was told when I graduated from high school that I could do one of two things: 1. Go to school or 2. Go to work. I opted to go to school. I graduated from Howard University in 1990 with a Bachelor's in Business Administration with a major in Finance. I was on a six-year program because I was one of those kids who just didn't know what she wanted to do. I went on to get a Graduate Degree from the City University of New York in Creative Writing. I was the person destined to get a good job, work for one company until I retired, and live well in my retirement with my grandchildren and hubby. You could say that I was on the path to living the American Dream.

But Momma and Daddy couldn't have prepared me for the world today: for the fact that our generation would have to struggle just to get half of the things they were able to attain, or that the job market would be so unpredictable that staying at one job for more than five years would be considered unusual. The world is a different place today. The job market is shrinking, but the population continues to increase steadily. And a staggering reality, revealed on the Oprah™ show, is that more than 70% of Americans are living paycheck to paycheck. If we want something different in this day and age, we have to do something different. For me, working in Corporate America while establishing and building a network marketing organization as a Plan B worked.

In March 2003, I knew that my future with the company that I was working for was limited when my mentor and boss got laid off. As a black woman working in Corporate America, I felt blessed to have someone serve as an advocate for me and my skills. My boss at the time would speak up for me and would fight to get me the best raises and bonuses, which I genuinely deserved. She was part of the reason I was able to earn a six-figure salary working in Corporate America. She played a major role in the promotions I received, and she assisted in helping me become an Assistant Director of Marketing. Back then, when she told me that she was being laid off, I cried. I was hurt, and quite frankly, I knew my corporate career was doomed.

At that time, I had been working my network marketing business for less than a year, but I quickly decided to re-dedicate myself to it. This would be my Plan B, because I knew that it was only a matter of time before I would be next to get laid off. Another year passed, and I was spared in that round of layoffs, but by March 2005, my time had come, and I didn't escape this particular round of cuts. I was let go along with 50 other people. By this time though, I knew that I could flourish in my network marketing business because my income had already crept up to the point where it virtually matched my corporate earnings. My husband and I were enjoying what he liked to call a "third income" in our household. So when my boss told me they were eliminating my position, I smiled, because I was so ready to go!

When I learned of my layoff, I was in the process of planning a big event that weekend with the CEO and Co-Founder of my network marketing company and the other consultants in the region, so I didn't have time to think about losing my job. All I could think about was being freed from Corporate. Dr. Martin Luther King's famous words "Free At Last, Free At Last, Thank God Almighty, I Was Free At Last!", were all that played in my head. No more of listening to a boss I couldn't stand. No more of playing by someone else's rules. No more pressure of faking that I was happy when in fact, I was not. I was elated.

I was happy and excited, and ready to take my network marketing business to another level. And that is exactly what I did. By the end of May 2005, I was promoted to Director in my network marketing company. This was a title that Corporate America refused to award me, only Assistant Director would do for them, but it didn't do it for me. And then just five months later, when our team's production for October 2005 beat October 2004's production by 600%, I was promoted to National Vice President and more than tripled my income. How is that for making a Quantum Leap?

I am excited to share what I have learned working in this industry. I know that anyone can make a Quantum Leap in their Network Marketing business if they do the same things that I did. Right now I am enjoying the freedom of being free from Corporate America! I'm living the life I've always imagined. I'm working from home, I'm available to my two small children, Taylor and Sasha, and I'm contributing to my household and community in a major way. Anyone who has the desire, commitment and passion can make a Quantum Leap in their network marketing business. And with this book, I set forth to show you how.

With more than 14 years experience in network marketing, I can tell you that you can re-invent your life in ways that you've never imagined with this industry. And with this book, I will demonstrate how this can happen for you. It doesn't matter if you're just getting started with a network marketing company or you're a seasoned network marketer looking to take your business to the next level. This book is for you. You are going to discover key principles and strategies that can shock your business to a new level of production. This is not an aggressive, in-your-face guide, but more of a comprehensive explanation of the truth about getting to the next level. It is my hope that every reader gets a clear sense and understanding that in this business there are no secrets. There are just facts and realities that everyone must face to move their business forward. Even if you're an entrepreneur, and not in the network marketing industry, this book can be useful to your business success.

My wish is that everyone who reads these pages finds something that will allow him/her to make that Quantum Leap, that irrefutable increase in your business, quantifiable with solid results, that will allow you to soar. Get excited about the possibilities! And get ready for your feet to rise off the floor. Get ready to soar. Are you ready? Say Yes!

Toni Coleman-Brown
Far Rockaway, NY
July 2006

Introduction

My Quantum Leap Story

When I decided to take my network marketing business to another level it felt as if I was beginning a Presidential campaign. I felt like I was running for the Oval Office. I knew that the team was ready to advance. I could tell by the energy and excitement of the organization. All of the key indicators were pointing to signs that it was time for us to move on up. In my particular compensation plan, getting documented at the top position is no minor feat. It requires 75 people to be positioned in the right place, and all must be active with a minimum of $500 in group sales volume. So, when I say that it felt like I was running for president, that's exactly what it was like. I had to rally all of those people together to achieve success.

Moving up in most compensation plans in network marketing is a team effort and as such it requires the support of the entire team. So I began early on rallying up the troops. A group of us decided that we all wanted to move up the plan during the month of October 2005. We sent out a call to action two months in advance and asked all those who wanted to go with us to raise their hands. The response was amazing. The vision was clear. We had more than enough people on board with plans of going to the next level. We had strategies in place to generate sales and to recruit new distributors. We made it fun. We had conference calls to strategize and to support each other in our efforts. By the time October 1st came, we all felt as if the promotions were a done deal. Everyone had their plans in action. The minimum amount of volume needed for the month of October in order for the promotion to happen was $72,500, and I knew that if we could generate half of that by the middle of the month, the promotion would definitely happen.

The month started out with a lion's roar. We worked! By the time we reached the mid-month checkpoint, we were halfway there. We had a huge training event planned for Oct. 17th and we were pumped. We had a huge turnout and signed on a lot of new people, further adding to our production for the month. But the last day of the month was a nightmare. It was October 31st, Halloween. It was our election night. All of the key players were on post standing by the phones and in front of their computers or out signing up people and working to make this promotion happen. At 3:00 in the afternoon, I was scared because I didn't see the numbers move and I was ready to throw in the towel. However, by the time I took my kids trick-or-treating, the numbers were moving steadily. I felt comfortable leaving the house. I went trick-or-treating and to a Halloween Birthday Party with my kids. They had a good time. When we arrived home later that night, we only a few orders away from our goal and I knew it was only a matter of time before it was over. By the time the clock struck midnight it was a done deal. All of the orders were not showing up on my computer system but all of them were accounted for on my spreadsheet. Yes. I kept a spreadsheet to keep track of it all.

The feeling of victory was better than anyone on the team could have imagined. I personally always wondered what it would feel like to document as a National Vice President.

I had dreamt of it when I first joined the company and there weren't any National Vice Presidents at all. When it officially happened for me, I received flowers from the corporate executive team, gifts from my upline sponsors and so many congratulatory wishes. It was over the top. It felt good. I wished that the feeling could last forever. The memory of that Quantum Leap will be forever etched in my mind. I will never forget the key players; they're names are written on the spreadsheet. I wish that I could say that they're all still in the game, but they're not. I understand that that's the nature of the business. But the good news is that even though some of them are not currently in the game, I still keep in touch with them because we have strong relationships.

I will never forget October 2005. Our team was unstoppable. Our chemistry was kinetic. Not only were we drawn to each other, but others were drawn to us as well and the same holds true today. Our sales were growing at a rapid pace and our recruiting was going through the roof. We were all excited to be a part of a winning team. It was amazing. We believed in each other and we believed in the team, but most importantly we believed that we were destined for success.

Success came to us that October with ease and grace. It was a sweat-less victory. There was no struggle at all. Some of us had the biggest checks ever. My own personal income more than tripled. Our theme song was "Going to Another Level" by Israel Houghton and the New Breed Choir. We definitely reached another level. The momentum continued in the following months. As I write this book, we're gearing up for another Quantum Leap in the upcoming months and it promises to be even better than before.

Going to the next level in your business requires certain actions. You have to master the basics, develop a certain mindset and become a fearless leader. Then once you've reached your goals, you have to have the courage, will and drive to set new goals and reach even higher. It's always about getting to the next level. It could be the next title or the next level of income, because ultimately everyone knows that when the amount of money you can earn is endless, you will make several Quantum Leaps within your network marketing career. The key is having the fortitude to stick it out until you've reached the top of that mountain. There are some key things that you must do to make a Quantum Leap in your network marketing business and the chapters ahead outline them all. Glean what you can from the information and make it your own.

Part I

Life Lesson

What does your future look like?

When you look into the future what do you see? A life that is beautiful and bright, filled with everything you've always hoped or a blank empty space because you've never thought about it?

Isn't it sad when you talk to people and you ask them what they see in the future and they don't know?

It's true there is a lot about our futures that we cannot control. But there is a lot about our futures that we can control as long as we take the appropriate steps and actions.

The funny thing is when you take time to visualize and see yourself in a different place, your body responds as if you're already there. Isn't that amazing? And the best part is that only your actions and decisions will keep you from getting there.

So decide now to take the right actions to paint the perfect picture for your future.

Toni Coleman Brown

Chapter 1

Start with the End in Mind

What is your vision for the future? Can you see yourself walking across the stage after your name has just been called as the Regional Vice President for XYZ company? What are you wearing? Who is in the audience? Is the crowd on their feet? How do you feel? What did you say to the audience?

Wow! That is an amazing picture, isn't it? I know some people have never visualized themselves reaching the top position in their companies. And some people think about it every day. Whatever your situation--you may not see yourself at the top position, but maybe as a Director or Sr. Manager or whatever the title is--the questions remains the same. Where do you see yourself? It doesn't matter what the answer is, but you must start working with this vision in mind.

You must work your business from the back to the front to make a Quantum Leap. In other words and you've heard it before, you must begin with the end in mind. Take a look at the compensation plan or marketing plan from your company and begin immediately building your business with the top or leading position in mind. Understand exactly what the qualifications are for the title you desire and you must begin to work with consistent premeditated actions that will allow this to happen.

Understand that when you decide to work your business from the top position down, you have made the first step that would put you on the path to reaching it. There is a saying, and the first time I heard it, I was at leadership training with Gloria Mayfield Banks, a top producing National with Mary Kay and Joanne Barnes, another top producing Mary Kay National and that saying is, "Inherent in the seed of the tree is the tree." What it means is simply this: Before a tree is planted, it is a seed, but when you plant the seed in the soil, is it not already a large oak tree? Indeed, it is. Even before it was watered and it bloomed, it was a tree, but in the form of a seed, most people can't see it as being a large beautiful oak tree that will provide lots of shade. Based on this analogy, isn't that seed (you) already at the top position of the plan? The answer is Yes. When you decide to go all the way to top, you must begin to act as if you're already there. You already are who you were meant to be or who you're going to be. It's just a matter of you deciding to walk in your destiny.

From a mindset perspective, you're already a National Vice President or Regional Vice President or Sr. RVP or whatever that top position is in your plan. It doesn't matter whether the documentation has caught up with you or not, that shouldn't stop you from beginning to act like that top performer. If there is someone currently at the top position in your network marketing company, begin to model that person. The beauty about this business is that you do not have to re-invent the wheel, you can just look at the actions of those who have already made it and duplicate their success. And when you duplicate them, duplicate just about everything.

What kind of car does the top producer drive? What kind of clothes do they wear? How do they speak? What kinds of things do they constantly talk about or promote? Pay close attention to these factors because success leaves clues all over the place and you want to pick up on every clue out there so you can duplicate it.

Copying someone is the highest form of flattery in this world, so trust me when I tell you that if you copy someone in network marketing who has had a tremendous amount of success, you will certainly not create an enemy: what you will create is a tremendous amount of wealth for yourself. It is powerful, but don't believe what I say, try it for yourself.

You want to be it until you see it, not fake it 'til you make it, because somehow, just the thought of "Faking It" brings negative energy and takes you out of balance with your true self, especially if you're the type of person who operates with honesty and integrity. You must literally be it until you see it in black and white. You have to be a top performer and top money earner in your mind until the paperwork catches up. When steps laid out in these chapters are followed, it doesn't have to take long to achieve your goals and that's the good news.

Starting your business with the end in mind is about having a clear vision for knowing where you're going, setting goals and following up with actions to help you get there. If you don't know where you're going, how can you realistically expect to get there? A dream is a goal without legs. You can dream all day long about where you want to go and what you want to do, but if you don't set specific targets and execute specific actions, then you will never go anywhere.

u # samples daily

21

Action is key. Action means acts in motion. And acts are specific deeds that are performed or executed. These feats get us closer to our goals.

Setting Your Goals

Langston Hughes asked the question, "Whatever happens to a dream deferred? Does it dry up like a raisin in the sun or does it fester like a sore and then run?" Dreams and visions of grandeur without goals and actions are like a car with a flat tire; they're both are going nowhere fast. In this business and in life you must set goals. Goals are like our personal (Global Positioning System) GPS units. You set the goal for the ending destination, while starting from where you are, and you are given step-by-step directions to get where you want to go. Life should be so simple, but unfortunately it is not. Therefore, instead of being given the steps to reach our goals, we must create them. This is what goal-setting is all about and this is also why many people never create them.

It takes time to set goals. You must write down what you want, why you want it, when you want to get it and what you're willing to do to get it. It is not a simple process, and it takes time. To effectively set goals for yourself, you should block out about four hours for each goal. As you can see, it will take days to properly set your goals. (See the goal-setting worksheet in the workbook section of this book) However, if you're serious about getting ahead, you will take the time to do so.

Break your goals up into manageable pieces or action steps. Have you ever gone online to get directions? You have to first enter your starting destination. Then enter your ending destination and then the system gives you directions in steps. Sometimes there are a few steps and sometimes there are hundreds of steps depending on where you're going. Sometimes there are one or two steps that last for many miles, which means that it will take you a while to move from that step to the next one. Setting and achieving goals are just like that. You literally become your own personal GPS unit.

Will you get lost on the journey to achieving your goals? Most likely. Will the directions be perfect? Not always. Nevertheless, you must always be prepared for when you get turned around or go down the wrong road. This is all a part of the process of getting where you want to go.

The one thing that is clear about becoming your own GPS unit is you must always start with the end in mind. Don't wait until you get to your destination to get excited. Get excited as soon as you get started. Visualize and experience the feelings of being on top every day and enjoy the journey of getting there.

Set your goals in 30-60-90 day intervals

Most corporations work their businesses in quarters. At the end of every quarter the boss receives quarterly results. The results of the previous quarter set the pace for the upcoming quarters, and in network marketing, it works the same way. Setting your goals in 30-, 60- and 90- day intervals will ensure that you have a business each month. Network marketing is not a business you can stop working for a minute. That is not to say that you cannot take a break. You can take a vacation, but just like being on a regular job, if you call yourself taking an extended vacation, you may find that you don't have a job when you return. The same holds true in this industry, you cannot stop working your business. The minute you do your business begins to quickly come to an end, unless you have well-developed leaders that will keep their business going. But that doesn't account for your own personal organization or the people you personally sponsored into the business, because they will drop off from lack of attention.

Three months is a manageable period of time for you to take a good look at your business and to begin to set goals that can and will take you to the top. It takes about 90 days for a good plan to kick into gear. Your goal is to be consistent with your activities and plans for those periods so your business can continuously grow and prosper.

Your network marketing goals should always revolve around selling, recruiting, marketing promotions, recognition and training events. Break down your sales goals into personal sales and team sales and for recruiting goals, do the same. Use the worksheets in the workbook section to help you set goals and track your activity. You will want to track for promotions and track for everyday success. Tracking and accountability is key to ensuring that the goals you set are being reached.

Personal goals are for you. It's not always necessary to share your personal goals with everyone. Sometimes you may want to keep them to yourself. These goals represent your innermost feelings, and it is okay if you want to keep them private. Some people enjoy shouting their goals to the world, and that's okay as well. You just have to figure out what type of person you are and how you want to handle your own personal goals.

Team goals are for everyone because everyone has an opportunity to participate in setting them. You now know that you cannot Quantum Leap by yourself, you must do it as a team. Therefore, you must set team goals based on where the team members have said that they want to go. Once you roll all the goals together, you have a clear vision for where you can go together. Team goals are about helping everyone go to the next level. It is okay to share the goals set by the team with everyone. It is interesting what happens to a team when everyone is plugged into the team goals and everyone knows what role they're to play in the team reaching its goals. When the team hits its target, everybody on that team wins. There is no better feeling than this. Nothing could be more exciting than everyone achieving more together. Have you ever seen a team win a championship game? It doesn't matter whether it's a little league game or a professional all-star team game. The tears of joy that are dropped for a team victory and those dropped in team defeat are always the same, meaning that no tear is more important than the other because everyone operated in unison and acted as team players.

The Bible says that "Without a Vision, the people will perish." Knowing where you and your team want to go gives your vision a foundation to stand on with targets and actions. One action at a time will get you closer to the vision. So having that picture of the end result will allow you to order your steps in that direction and win.

Life Lesson

Everyday You Get a Fresh Start

Every time you wake up in the morning you're given a
Fresh Start, a clean slate, ready for a new story to be
written or a new song to be sung.
Isn't it great that every day you get the chance to re-invent
yourself all over again?
Who will you be today?
Who have you become?
We are the sum of all of our past experiences, but the
equation is not complete…there is still time to multiply and
bring forth the harvest.
Today is that day. It is a day of new beginnings. It is time
to re-write that chapter and this time change the ending.

Toni Coleman Brown

Chapter 2

Make a Decision and Let Go of the Outcome

The word "decision" is derived from the word incision, which means to cut off. Therefore when you decide something in your mind, you must cut off the possibility of anything else occurring. A key to making your Quantum Leap is deciding that this is what you want to do. Once you make this decision, you must release any other thoughts. For example, if you have decided that you're going to become a top-producing National or Regional Vice President in your organization (or whatever the top position is), becoming a Director or Senior Director is not good enough. You should not stop until you have hit the top position of National or Regional Vice President because this is what you have made up your mind to do.

What does this mean? It means that quitting is not an option. Not only is it not an option, it is not a word that even exists in your vocabulary. Failing is also not an option. Not getting what you want is not an option. Losing the game is not an option. Once you've decided to go to the next level in your business, the only option you have is to succeed. Period.

A decision for the most part is absolute. Imagine being on trial and hearing the verdict. Once the verdict is rendered (a decision has been made), it is pretty much definite unless you appeal. And that is what happens to most of us in life. We make a decision to do something and instead of cutting off all the possibilities of anything else occurring, we begin to make appeals or compromises. The bottom line is that these compromises are nothing more than excuses and there is no room for them in your life when you get on the path toward success.

Letting go of the outcome of your decision means that you're not going to get hung up when or if everything doesn't go exactly as you planned and that you're going to keep moving toward your goal no matter what. Recognize that you cannot control the outcome, but know that when the universe aligns itself with your decision, it will happen. It must happen. Unusual circumstances will happen in your organization. Everything will not always be perfect. Your company will not be perfect. Your company cannot be everything for everyone, nor should it strive to be. No company could survive if it decided to please everyone. Once you have decided which company you're going to go all the way with, there is nothing left for you to do except do it. You will have to go through good times and bad, good corporate decisions and bad ones. However none of this will matter because you understand that your success is not based on corporate decisions. It is based on you.

The decision process to move up is the same as what you experienced when you signed on the dotted line to become an independent representative. You knew that you wanted to be a success. You were excited, energetic and ready to learn all there is to know about your new business. Then life happens or the appeals begin to happen. The appeals are the obstacles or stumbling blocks that get in the way of your desire to go to the next level. This is why you have to let go of the outcome as to how you think you're going to get to the next level because often, how you think your jump to the next level is going to happen is not necessarily the way it does.

For example, you get started in a new business or you decide that you're going to take your faltering business to another level. You have this great idea that your family and friends are going to participate at your same level of excitement about what you know is about to happen for everyone who joins your business. You see yourself moving up and you already have the names of your family and friends who will support you and your new venture. However when you reach out to them, the opposite occurs. The very people you expected to support you are the ones who are the most negative. But it doesn't matter what anyone says about what you're doing. You're going to see it through. It doesn't matter if they laugh at you, if they don't support you, or if they think you've gone crazy. It doesn't matter. All that matters is that you have made a "decision" that you're committed to seeing through to the end.

Something empowering happens to people when they start network marketing businesses. There is something about making this decision that makes people walk with a different stride and talk with a certain level of confidence. Maybe that's what intimidates their friends and family because God forbid these new reps do something that will put them in a better category than their family members or friends. Nevertheless, there is definitely a transformation that occurs. New reps no longer think or act like the people they used to be. Folks will go from being Casscius Clay to Muhammed Ali. The old person dies and a new life is born with a new attitude. And it happens in a split second or at least it seems this way.

Men will go from being Clark Kent to Superman. Women will go from being Diana Prince to Wonder Woman. That's the feeling of empowerment and it comes with the territory. With a new found energy and strength, you'll feel as if you can conquer the world, and the beauty of this is the fact that… You Can!

As a new rep, you should savor the feeling you had when you first became a representative, and you should remember your reasons for joining your organization, because you're going to have to draw on that same excitement and energy for your entire career. You will be able to use your why as a motivator for getting started with your business month after month. You will use your why to re-recruit yourself into the business every 30 or 31 days.

Your journey to the top of your company begins the minute you become a distributor, but you don't get on the road to making a Quantum Leap and going to the top until you decide it's time. Let's be clear here, hundreds even thousands of people join network marketing companies every day, but those who make it to the top and make the Quantum Leaps do so because they've made up their minds to do just that. Once a person's mind is made up to do something though, there is nothing left for them to do, except Do It!

You should know that before you can soar or have victory in anything you do in life that there is a price that must be paid. There is pain and suffering that occurs on the road to any victory. Just think about a time when you've worked out, and attempting to get a new body, you had to make sacrifices. For some people it may have meant getting up a couple of hours earlier to exercise, eating right and writing down everything they ate. Making a Quantum Leap in this business is not much different from that. You will have to make sacrifices to get to the next level. It will take hard work and long hours and if anyone tells you that it will be any different, they're telling you a bold-face lie. This price will be paid upfront. You will have to work hard over a relatively short period of time to have a long-term gain.

That short period may be one to seven years or maybe longer, depending on the level of energy you put into your business. Most people start network marketing companies part-time and work up to the point in which they can go full-time. The more seasoned a company becomes, the longer it may take for new people to reach the top position of the company because of saturation. However, some people come into relatively seasoned companies and jet to the top of their plans when they follow the systems in place. Nevertheless, it is not unheard of for a person to take seven or more years to make it to the top of a marketing plan and quite honestly that is not a long period of time. If you don't believe it, just ask anyone over 40. Since the time is going to pass by anyway, you might as well do something that will have a huge impact on your life and possibly change the history of your family.

Do not worry or concern yourself with the outcome. Often, when people are running for a promotion or to get to the next level, they tend to get fixated on a particular group of people helping them to get there. For example, Susan Polk* was seeking a promotion in her company and the promotion called for three people to get to a certain level. Susan was certain that she was going to get this promotion because she had already recruited three people and she was convinced that they were all on fire. They had told her their goals at the beginning of the month and she proceeded to work her business with full confidence that she was going to make it. In the middle of the month, one of her key players, called her to say that she had been diagnosed with a serious illness and she would no longer be available to work her business because she had to begin treatments right away. While Susan was devastated at the news of her condition, she was also concerned and afraid that she would not meet her promotion goal. She didn't quit her pursuit though. She sent flowers to her former rep and a word of sympathy, and she continued to work her business. At one of her parties, two of the guests were so excited with Susan's presentation, they signed on right on the spot. They both worked their business in the little amount of time they had left in the month, which allowed Susan not only to qualify for the promotion, but she skipped the goal that she was aiming for and reached a higher title. Susan was overjoyed with her results.

If Susan had kept her mind fixated on the reaching her goal with the three people she started the month with on her team, she would have been disappointed and probably would have stop working towards her goal when she got some bad news. However, she let go of the outcome and continued to work on reaching her goal with the full expectation of achieving it, and not only did she achieve it, she surpassed it. Her story is a powerful testimony to what happens when individuals become determined to succeed. She understood that things do not always happen the way you plan them. However, utilizing the law of expectancy, she was guaranteed a win.

The Law of Expectancy is linked to what was explained earlier because it shows what happens when you make a "decision" to win. You fully expect to do so and no other possibilities exists in your mind. It's a powerful universal law and it demonstrates the awesome power of a mind made up. It's just like the game show, "Who Wants to Be a Millionaire" when the host asks, "Is That Your Final Answer?" and you respond "That Is My Final Answer." When your mind is made up, there is no turning back. When you decide that going to the top is what you want to do, it doesn't matter if it takes you 10, 20 or 30years, you will do it. It may happen with a totally different team than the one you have now, but if you expect it to happen, it will.

Life Lesson

An Entrepreneur's Creed

E – Everything is done in a spirit of Excellence.
N – Never give up.
T – Time is priceless, so use it with care.
R – Respect the customer because he is right.
E – Everything is possible for those who believe.
P – Passion for what you do is mandatory.
R – Repetition helps to master one's skill.
E – Experience is not necessary, but hard work is.
N – Not succeeding is NOT an option.
E – Expand your territory through word of mouth.
U – Unique selling proposition sets you apart
R – Rest because you must, but never quit.

By Toni Coleman Brown

Chapter 3

Develop the Mindset of a Business Owner

As an independent representative, you are the owner of your own network marketing distribution center with representatives across the countries and continents (if your company is international), and you will want to run your business as such. This is the area in which most representatives fall short. Most people who come into this industry have no clue as to what they've signed up for. Even though the network marketing business model is different from most other traditional businesses, they must be operated in the same way.

A friend of mine, Tracey, decided she wanted to start her own business baking cakes. She had recently been laid off from her job, and no one could understand why she had no desire to go back to work in Corporate America. Some people asked, "Tracey, are you crazy? You have all of those skills and all of that education and you're going to throw it all away to bake cakes! You've completely lost your mind." Tracey didn't pay attention to any of the naysayers. She began to work day and night to get her cake business off the ground. She began marketing, giving away samples and testers so she could get orders. For the holiday season, her phone rang off the hook. She could barely handle all the orders. She was overflowing with business. Her cake business was taking off. She spent many sleepless days and nights baking cakes, fulfilling orders, and writing a business plan so she could grow her business. She worked tirelessly. While others were asleep, Tracey was up working on her business because she could see herself one day on *Oprah* or in a famous magazine as becoming a successful entrepreneur.

Tracey's drive, vision and tireless efforts are the same as those required for a network marketing entrepreneur. As a matter of fact, Tracey gained a lot of her business acumen from working a network marketing business. Most people look at entrepreneurs as being crazy while others look at them in sheer amazement. They ask questions like "Have you lost your mind?" especially if the entrepreneurs gave up good jobs or careers to follow their dreams and pursue the life of working on their own. If your family and friends give you problems or talk about you behind your back when you begin your business, don't worry. It's not because they don't love you, it's because they simply do not understand.

Entrepreneurs are special people. Professional networkers definitely fall into this category. An entrepreneur has vision for the future. This person can see things that other people cannot. They have the eyesight of an eagle. What they can see perfectly clear at 2000 feet, most people could not see it if it were directly in front of their faces. These people have unshakable faith and belief. They understand what it means to step out on faith. They know that faith is the evidence of things hoped for and the substance of things not yet seen. Most people who don't have an entrepreneurial mindset cannot see anything because they're too busy trading time for money. They're used to trading dollars for hours or working X hours for Y pay. Unlike most entrepreneurs, they can't understand the concept of working hard on the front end so that you can get paid generously on the back end.

Most business plans project businesses to operate at a loss in the first couple of years before they begin to break even and generate income. But the average person doesn't know or understand this concept. All they know or understand is that they work set hours and get set pay and they can't understand how they can come into a business like this and work extremely hard and not make a great deal of money right away. They think "I don't work this hard at my job but they earn XX dollars every two weeks." These people get confused when they begin working their network marketing businesses, and they get frustrated and quit. That's because they don't have an entrepreneurial mindset and they don't know anything about running their own business.

You must always remember that you are network marketing professionals, which means that you are an entrepreneur and business owner. You live in a different world and you operate with a different mindset. Don't become discouraged when others don't see things your way. Understand that being an entrepreneur can be lonely. There is nothing worse than having a clear vision for where you're going and others don't get it or see it or worse, don't believe it. It's hard to be on a team and be motivated and have a clear vision for where you want to go and what you want for your team members and to have them not understand or have limited belief in where you are going. Some entrepreneurs get frustrated and discouraged during these times, but remember entrepreneurs see things that others cannot and must stay strong and persevere even when others do not share the vision.

Being an entrepreneur is also a state of mind. Entrepreneurs live with an overall attitude of positive expectancy. They just expect the best. They expect positive results. They expect to win. They see the glass as being half full instead of half empty.

They don't buy into other people's opinions of them because they know that when you buy into other's opinions, you buy into their lifestyle. Most people are negative and miserable and if you want to be negative and miserable, all you have to do is keep listening to them. Entrepreneurs don't do that. As a matter of fact, entrepreneurs cut themselves off from all negativity, and that includes negative people. Entrepreneurs understand the need to associate with positive people.

Now that you have a clear understanding of what it takes to develop the mindset and viewpoint of an entrepreneur, you want to develop a business plan. See below for a sample of what this business plan could look like.

**Business Plan Template
(for Your Network Marketing Business)**

Introduction

I am an independent consultant/distributor of_____. It is the purpose of this business plan to outline the foundation of my business. This document lays out my vision, philosophy and strategy. It will serve as a guideline for the present and future strategies for making my business run efficiently and profitably.

Business Overview

Where will your business be located? (Be specific as to which room in your home and how much space you will allot yourself. This is important at tax time.)_____

What are your general short- and long-term goals? (This should be 2 sentences max.)

_____

_____

What is your main strategy for reaching your goals? (Again, keep this short. You will have a chance to elaborate later.)

_____

_____

_____

What past work or life experiences will be beneficial to your success, and why?

_____

_____

_____

Target Market

What is your target (focus) market? (i.e. age range, sex, income level, etc.)_____

What are the market needs that you plan to meet?_____

How do you plan to reach your market? (Ads, website, opportunity meetings? Be as specific as possible and include details)

_____

_____

_____

What are your marketing goals?

(How many leads would you like to generate per week or per month?)_____

What would you say are the advantages of *Your Company* over other plans/companies (your competitors?) out there, and how do you plan to leverage that in your marketing?_____

What is your advertising budget? (Make sure you fill out the cash flow worksheet so that you don't overspend!)

How much do you intend to spend on advertising and when do you plan to advertise? (monthly ads, yearly ads, sporadic, etc.)

Financial Projections

What are your financial goals Short-term? _____Long-term?_____

How will you generate your profits? (direct sales, team level overrides or both?)_____

How many parties/shows, vending events, 1:1's, presentations, etc., do you plan on doing each month? How much do you think your commissions will be on these activities? _____

What other methods will you use to sell your products? (trade shows, lunchroom or office presentations, etc.)_____

What are your sponsoring or recruiting goals per week, month, year?_____

How many consultants do you plan on directly sponsoring to reach that goal?

How will you ensure a continuation of profits over time?

_____

_____

_____

Additional Business Plan Worksheets

Start-Up Costs

Start-Up kit (incl. S&h and taxes)	
Office Supplies (pens, folders, labels)	
Advertising	
Business Supplies (business cards, etc.)	
Long Distance & phone	
Misc.	

Cash Flow Projection Worksheet

Income	Jan	Feb	Mar	Apr	May	Jun	Jul	Aug	Sep	Oct	Nov	Dec	Total
Personal Commissions													
Team Overrides													
Bonuses													
Total													

Monthly Expense Projection Worksheet

Expenses	Jan	Feb	Mar	Apr	May	Jun	Jul	Aug	Sep	Oct	Nov	Dec	Total
Office Supplies													
Business supplies (catalogs, invitations, hostess & success brochures)													
Advertising													
Kit additions													
Gas													
Parking													
Tolls													
Mileage													
Airfare-Travel													
Meals/Food/Hotel													
Events/Conference													
Phone/Cell bill													
Internet Site													
Vending Table Cost													
TOTAL													

Branding Your Organization

Establish a name for your team the moment you become documented at the first leadership title in your company (or the title that entitles you to begin earning leadership bonuses), begin promoting your team in your network marketing community. Your organization is your asset. It doesn't matter if it consists of 100 people or thousands of people, you will want to begin to brand it. Branding is a huge step toward starting to treat your business like a business. Building a strong team brand will help you to become successful. You will form an identity that will transcend the company whose products you market.

For example, let's say the name you decided to choose for your organization is X-Factor Marketing, LLC, and you begin to promote this brand heavily. You also start to venture off into other venues with X-Factor Marketing and the brand becomes so strong that people in other network marketing companies begin to recognize you. If one day you may have to leave your current company because something out of your control happens, if you've built a strong team brand, your entire team may decide to come with you because you've built strong faith and belief in the team. This is exactly what you want to happen in your business.

Understand that branding is something that happens over a period of time. However, in establishing your team brand and name identity, you will want to start by creating a supportive organizational culture right from the start. This will be the manner in which your team operates. You will want to set high ethical standards and insist that everyone operates within those standards or leave. You will also want to set the standards for production. You will want to set your production standards high so new people coming on board will understand what is expected of them. You will also want to set your mission and vision as well so everyone on the team knows where the team is headed and what everyone is working toward. And to create team spirit, you can develop motivational tools like a team chant. These things are critical when establishing your team brand.

Creating a team and brand identity will help you stand out in the crowd. Determine what your team will be known for and be consistent with your message. This will create a wow factor, which sets your team apart from others in the organization. Others in the industry will come to know your team by the brand, and recognize what you've accomplished and how you've broken records.

While your team leaders or your business builders will begin to develop their own brands within your brand, it is important to always emphasize the larger team because this will be important for corporate functions, when you will want your team together as a united front representing one brand. This will further emphasize the strength of the brand. Your business builders' brands should always continue to promote and represent the larger team brand as its core.

Life Lesson

"Success is going from failure to failure without losing your enthusiasm."

Author: Winston Churchill

Chapter 4

You Will Wear Many Hats

As a business owner, you are going to wear many hats. I like to equate owning a business to the game of football. In business you will wear the hat of Business Owner, Team Player, Motivator and Team Leader; in football, these would be the roles of Franchise Owner, Team Player, Coach, and Quarterback, respectively. You will have to learn how to master all these different roles to have a successful organization.

Let's start with the Business Owner or in football Franchise Owner hat. As the owner of the business, you are expected to do a lot of things. You must:

- Make sure the team Operates at a certain level financially.
- Ensure that all the players are satisfied with their contracts and agreements.
- Track all of your reports and report back.

Therefore as a Business Owner, you will make sure your business is running at an optimal level. You will do this by asking yourself some key questions that will determine whether or not you're running a healthy business. Most of these questions will be directly related to your company's compensation plan. You're going to want to know the number of new people you're signing on to your business, how many people are active, and if your number of active distributors is increasing or decreasing? You will also want to see if your team members are moving up the comp plan? You are going to constantly look for ways to analyze your business so you can find ways to stimulate your results through incentives and team promotions. You will not be able to do this however if you don't have a clear understanding of your team's sales behavior. You will also want to put together tracking sheets to help track your results. If you track something like daily sales, you can put together some curves that may allow you to statistically determine and project what your sales will be for the month after the first five days or so have passed. Corporations use these types of sophisticated statistical models all the time to project results. You can do the same thing.

When you have on your Business Owner hat, you are watching the game (your team's production) from an aerial view. You have to put your special lens on your glasses so you can see things that your team members may not. You will be able to guide them into promotions or help them develop personally. The Business Owner has an all-knowing eye and is able to put together short-term and long-term strategies for growth and profitability.

The Business Owner hat is a favorite of mine because it places you in the same category as traditional brick and mortar business owners. More often than not after careful analysis of your business revenue, you will find that you have generated more sales than a traditional business owner in the same 12-month period.

Therefore, it is a fine hat to where in network marketing and probably one of the most difficult for network marketers to wear because of the lack of business experience in the representatives. Sometimes when reps do have experience in business, it limits them as network marketers because they can't understand the concept of having leverage by building a team. This happens often because they're used to working alone. It is also difficult for many people to transition into the role of Business Owner because they approach the business with the wrong mentality. These people are looking for a paycheck, when they've only done the work to get a "playcheck".

It takes time to develop the qualities necessary to wear the hat of a Business Owner, however, with some practice, knowledge and mastering of skills, it can happen. And before long, the average person is mapping out strategies for long-term and short-term profitability and finding that they can operate successfully.

Another hat you will wear is that of the Team Player. T.E.A.M. – Together Everyone Achieves More! How many times have you heard this concept in network marketing? Probably hundreds but what does it actually mean? It's a tall statement and you have to reach high to grasp it completely.

Most network marketers don't understand that when they decide to become independent consultants, they are immediately becoming members of a larger team as well. The independent consultant becomes a player on a team that represents the entire company and from that point on he or she represents the founders, top producers, and the other representatives in that company. Therefore, it is in the network marketer's best interest to arm him or herself through training with the information necessary to become a powerful representative of that company, everything that the independent consultant says or does will permanently impact the reputation of the company.

Think about professional sports, like the NFL and NBA and how they require players to attend all games and to travel in business suits. This was challenged at one time because some players wanted to be "mavericks" and represent their own urban style. However, this was quickly put down because the corporate organizations felt as if they had a standard to uphold and they wanted the players to reflect this standard of professionalism. It is the same way with network marketing. The representatives must reflect the professional standards set forth by the corporate leaders. They must be team players.

A team player must learn all aspects of the business. In sports, just because you represent a particular position, you still have to learn the job of all the other players on the team. The same holds true in network marketing. If you have promoted to a particular title or position in your company and it is not the top position of the company, does that mean that it's okay for you to operate as if you don't know what the person in the top position has to do? No. It is in your best interest to learn what the top leader does as well. How will you ever reach the top level status if you don't know what they had to do to get there?

Team players shows up and participate in all major meetings and functions. They understand all aspects of putting together a business opportunity meeting. They raise their hands and volunteer to assist in every way necessary.

Team players have good ethics and operate in an ethical fashion. They don't lie or steal or make false promises. They don't sign-up other people's prospects. They understand that each team player represents the team as a whole and that if one person is not playing fair then it throws off the synergy of the entire team.

Then there is the hat of the Team Leader. The team leader is the go-to person. In football, this would be the quarterback. If the team leader isn't present and participating in all aspects of the game, then the entire organization suffers.

Just like everyone follows the lead of the quarterback, the same holds true for leaders in network marketing. You have to lead the pack. As a leader, you must lead by example. Otherwise, your organization will be in conflict. If you say one thing and do something else, your organization will suffer. For example, you cannot tell your team to register for an event, if you are not registered. How can you tell someone to sell $1,000 in product when you don't do it.

A team leader should have integrity. If you are not someone who people can trust then it will be hard for you to establish relationships with people. Integrity is not something you can earn or something you can pick up overnight by reading a book. Integrity is something that is inside of you. It means being a person of your word, saying what you mean and meaning what you say. The important thing about integrity is that once it is lost, it is very hard to build back up. Therefore, it is important to maintain a high level of integrity at all times.

A team leader is humble, not cocky or arrogant and never brags about his/her personal success to team members. Interestingly enough, network marketing is an industry in which you cannot advance without a team, even though there are various clubs and honors you can receive on your own based on your own personal production. However, what good does it do to have your name up in lights if none of your team member's names are up there with you. It is important to cultivate an environment in your organization where everyone achieves. And the more you help your team members achieve, the better off you will be. Help them to achieve success and you will achieve success. If however you achieve success and constantly brag and boasts about all you have done in your team member's faces, that will cause an environment of resentment versus one of high team spirit. While it is important to lead by example, sometimes you might need to take a back seat for a minute to provide navigation and leadership so that your team members can drive the organization to success.

A team leader is everything to everyone. You are there to serve your team members. Never forget that. Your team needs you. They need your expertise, your guidance and experience. And your role is to make sure that you are accessible enough for them to receive it.

You will also wear the hat of Motivator, or the Coach on a sports team. The Coach is the master motivator and inspirer. This person understands and inspires the team to Quantum Leap. Motivation normally comes from within. Motivation in network marketing comes from an individual's compelling vision. What the Motivator sees for the future keeps them moving toward that goal day by day. However, if you, as the Motivator, finds someone who doesn't see anything in his/her future, your role is to help them paint that picture of what their future could hold.

If you look at all the different hats you wear and put them together, they're like the perfect football season. Your home parties and in-home opportunity meetings are like your Pre-Season Games. Your business presentations and your business opportunity meetings represent your Regular Season Games, and your big meetings are like your Play-off games. And finally, your Regional Trainings and Sales events are like your Regional Championship Games and the National events are like the Superbowl, where you're going for the championship ring. Everyone should be present and accounted for at your organizations National events because this is where the team will receive all of its glory and accolades. That annual recognition is what drives continued success for the next season in the business and encourages everyone to strive on. Overall you will want to make sure that every season is filled with success.

Life Lessons

"To avoid criticism do nothing, say nothing, be nothing."

Author: Elbert Hubbard

Chapter 5

Become a Fearless Leader

There are so many qualities that define a leader. You could probably list over a thousand adjectives and they would all correctly describe a leader because a leader is everything to everyone.

A fearless leader is not afraid to take risks. Leaders understand that they may not always do or say the right things, but at the end of the day there will be lessons learned, and true leaders understand that real growth is in the lessons learned. This way, there is no such thing as failure. There are only life lessons. So you take a risk and make a mistake. Is it a failure? No, because mistakes are not failures. Mistakes are just obstacles in the way of success. A true leader understands that this is a natural part of being successful. Therefore he/she doesn't fear taking a risk because he/she knows that at the end of the day, there is a big return waiting in the process.

A fearless leader is not afraid to sometimes stand alone. Leaders understand the meaning of sometimes being a maverick. They may not say or do the things that others agree with, but they don't bother with the opinions of others because they walk to the beat of their own drums. They understand that it is okay to at times walk away from the crowd and they accept this challenge with honor.

A fearless leader is not afraid to tell the truth. Sometimes the truth can be a painful reality. It's like in the scene in *A*

Few Good Men when Jack Nicholson says, "You Want the Truth, You Can't Handle the Truth." Most people can't handle the truth. Network marketing forces everyone to take a long hard look in the mirror and face the many issues that they've spent years trying to cover up. Most people can't handle that. They can't handle the reality of seeing themselves for who they are. In this business people often have a tendency to compare themselves to others, but there is no reason to do that when the real comparison is with you yourself. Leaders, especially during 1:1 coaching, are faced with the question, "What am I doing wrong?" When you're in a position answer this question honestly, you do the person asking a real dis-service if you don't answer truthfully. A leader must be honest and let team members know what they're doing wrong, even when it's not an easy conversation. Everyone is better off when you tell the truth.

A fearless leader is not afraid of success. Success is such a relative thing. It means different things to different people. A child growing up to adulthood has major success all throughout life. They learn to talk, walk, etc. And they are not afraid to do it. Children are not afraid to make mistakes or take risks. They thrive on the positive feedback that success has to offer. Grown-ups, on the other hand, tend to fear being successful. They're afraid of what others might think, so they go through life playing small, never seeking to outshine anyone, always looking to fade to black or fall in the backdrop. As a human being and child of God, you should know that being successful is your destiny and there is no need to fear it, but every reason to embrace it. Not just embrace it though... enjoy it and relish in it as if it is an everyday part of life. If the average person looks over his/her life, I bet they would find a million successes that they've experienced. But because their names are not Oprah Winfrey or Bill Gates, they believe that they're not successful. It is a shame that most Americans define success by the amount of *things* a person has. Success comes in many packages, and we shouldn't fear it at all.

A fearless leader is never scared. That is a crazy sentence. But there was a rap group that had a song and the hook on the song was "I ain't never scared." As a leader in network marketing you will come to know and understand those lyrics in ways you never thought you would. Network marketing can be a very volatile industry. It has its peaks and valleys. As a leader in this industry you cannot afford to show fear. You are the one person who everyone is looking up to. Your wind always has to blow in a positive direction, no matter what. And as a leader, you must be willing to accept that challenge.

I have heard people say some interesting things about fear. I've heard that fear is the result of false evidence that appears real. I've heard that fear is the opposite of faith. And I've heard that on the other side of fear is freedom. Even after hearing these things, I still believe that fear is real. It is a real emotion you experience. But you have to walk through it. This is where you put your friends called faith and belief on notice and let them know that you will be leaning on them for a while.

As a leader looking to go to the next level with your company, your faith and belief have to be so strong that nothing makes you afraid. You must believe and have faith in your company, products, service, team, leaders, compensation plan, knowing that they can and will deliver...No Matter What!

As a fearless leader you can overcome any situation and you understand that the key to your success lies within you, not the company. If you have faith and belief, you can Quantum Leap even in a horrible network marketing company because you understand that it's not about what they do, it's about what you do as a leader. It doesn't matter what the company is doing wrong, it's all about what you're doing right and what you're promoting as a leader who is fearless.

Fearless leaders drive sales in network marketing. They are number one money-earners, they break company records, and they never stop because they're unstoppable.

Life Lesson

"You give but little when you give of your possessions. It is when you give of yourself that you truly give."

Author: Khalil Gibran

Chapter 6

Develop An Amen Corner

When you get on the path to success, beware of other people's opinions! Do not listen to them, especially those of negative people. For those negative people are going nowhere fast. Wherever you find negative people in 2005, rest assured they will be right in the same spot in 2006, and again in 2007 and certainly nothing will change for them in 2008 or at any other time in the future. When you buy into the opinions of negative people, you buy right into their lifestyle and if those folks, and it doesn't matter who they are--husband, boyfriend, girlfriend, mom or dad– are not living the lifestyle that you desire, then you need to run. You need to run as if your life depended on it, because guess what? It does!

Now imagine this character, let's call him Uncle Buddy. Uncle Buddy is sitting in his regular spot preaching to you about everything that you're doing wrong and what you should be doing and how you should be doing it. Let's call his banter "Life According to Uncle Buddy". He's talking and talking and talking and saying some intelligent things too. You would think that Uncle Buddy has his act together. But he has been doing his soap box ministry for years and every year Uncle Buddy's situation stays the same. You sometimes wonder why he never takes his own advice. Take a real good look at him. Is he living the way you want to live? Is Uncle Buddy dressed the way you want to dress? Does he smile the way you want to smile?

Does he laugh the way you want to laugh? If the answer to these questions is No, then you do not want to listen to Uncle Buddy.

That's the problem with most of us. We get too caught up listening to the Uncle Buddies of the world. At some point in our lives we have to be big boys and girls and trust our own judgment to do what's right for us and to make our own decisions. Therefore, when you decide to become the President and CEO of your own network marketing company, you want to remove the possibility of ever looking back on your decision, but more importantly, you want to remove the Uncle Buddies of the world from your circle, so they cannot influence you in a way that might make you want to re-think or fall back on your decision.

Your family and friends love you and genuinely do not want to see you fall prey to something that might not be good for you, but sometimes they're just afraid of those things that they do not understand. And instead of encouraging you to go out and do your best, they tend to say things to make fun of what they don't understand. Napoleon Hill, the author of *"Think and Grow Rich"* said it best when he said that, ""Close friends and relatives...often handicap one through 'opinions' and...ridicule...meant to be humorous. Thousands of men and women carry inferiority complexes with them all through life, because some well-meaning but ignorant person destroyed their confidence through 'opinions' or ridicule." You must learn to quiet this noise, so it doesn't distract you on your journey.

It is so important to have a support system while in the industry. This business is a people business and people will bring to you all sorts of problems and issues and can drain your energy. People in your presence will either give you energy or steal all of your energy and you will need every ounce of energy you have to make a Quantum Leap. Because of this, it is mandatory that you develop a support system.

As a leader, you will give so much to everyone on your team, as well as folks on the outside of your team and this will take a lot out of you. As a result you will need a place or person or group of people that you can go to fill you up with what you need to push through. You cannot give all of yourself and expect to have some leftover for you if you don't develop an outlet that provides an uplifting of the spirit.

Network marketing can be competitive, sometimes cutthroat. You may have moments in which you feel there is no one you can trust with your true feelings or nowhere you can go to freely express exactly what and how you feel. Your upline has a vested interest in you and they want you to produce, so their view of what you should or shouldn't do will be tainted. You also cannot readily go to your downline for help because they may be de-motivated or shocked by the reality that their own leader needs coaching and inspiration. So where does one go, especially if they have a negative spouse or partner who doesn't understand the business or the industry? The best thing to do in cases like these is to find someone outside of your circle, but inside the industry, or at least knows something about network marketing, to help guide you in the right direction or provide you with the inspiration you need to stay on track.

Get a coach. Coaching is a great thing and there are so many offerings and opportunities to get what you need from people in the industry who have experience in network marketing. When I decided to make a Quantum Leap in my company, I got a coach. All great performers have great coaches to help them get to the top of their game. A coach cannot do the work that is necessary for you to have success, but a coach can inspire you and guide you to the appropriate actions necessary for you to have success. A coach can be that Amen corner you need to cheer you on all the way to the top. Through analysis and exploration, a coach will guide you and find all the right buttons to push to help you succeed.

Create a Mastermind Group of your peers. This is an awesome way to brainstorm new ideas and concepts to help you Quantum Leap. The Mastermind group will serve as a sounding board for letting off steam. Make sure that your group consists of individuals with the same mindset and those who are committed to move in the same direction.

Pick people with care. Make sure that those who you choose to support you have your best interest at heart. Don't believe that just because a person is in the business with you or because you're a part of someone's downline that that person is your friend. That individual may be the one who smiles at you and applauds you the most, but secretly wishes you fail. I have seen it happen all too often, where a person is "acts" like a friend to a fellow consultant, and the consultant confides in the person and tells her every secret of her soul, and while that person may seem to be fully on your side, as soon as you leave their sight, they're damning your name. It is so hard to peg these types of individuals because they seem so sincerely on your side. The best way to conquer this is to limit the people you allow into your personal circle and know when to cut off a conversation.

Seek to avoid negativity and gossip at all cost. There is no room in an organization for this at all, but it always seems to rear it's ugly head in business. It is just as important to curtail your level of gossip and negativity, as it is to crush it when it presents itself to you. It is imperative to your growth, success and energy level that you surround yourself with positive people. If you allow negative folks to invade your space, you will find yourself sinking into a hole that is hard to come out of. Gossip can have a damaging impact on your team. And while it is easy to fall into a conversation that leads to gossip, it is so important to pull out before the conversation goes there. I know this from personal experience. One time I said something to someone in my business who told it to someone else, who went back and told it to the person that I spoken of, and the worst part was then the person I spoke about repeated the information to me and said, "I don't know where so-and-so got that from." And boy did I feel like crap. Not only could this have ruined my relationship with that person, but it could have negatively impacted our business. It is so important to leave gossip and negativity behind because it slows momentum. Instead, you want to fuel your business and team with positive inspiration and powerful people.

Go to church. The church is a great place to get filled and to find the message you might need to take back to your team. The church can give you the uplifting that you might need to make your Quantum Leap. There is no better place to find an Amen corner than in a church. More often than not, you will receive more information at church that can help you leap to the next level than you can obtain anywhere else. This is because the message that you often receive in church helps you to build belief in yourself and your business. There is nothing better than leaning on the promises of God and knowing that you are destined for success. Most often, the message of the church is one of good news, thanksgiving and praise. It helps you build your belief in people, in life and in the world around you. This is so important when it comes to building a business. Especially after you've had a rough week of dealing with people, being able to fellowship with other like-minded individuals is a blessing. Surrounding yourself with positive people is essential for sustainability in this industry and critical if you want to go to the next level. It is not just recommended it is essential.

Learn to Manage Your Emotions

Managing your emotions is, by far, one of the most critical skills a network marketer must acquire to make a Quantum Leap. Let's face it, life is emotional and this is an emotional business; as such, it just makes sense to try and understand one of the most critical aspects of the business.

Why do most people become a part of network marketing business? People usually join because someone said something touched an emotion in them. Something struck a cord with them when the speaker gave his presentation. The new recruit wanted a better life for himself and his family. He felt like something was missing from his life and that this (business opportunity) could fill the gap. The new recruit based his decisions on feelings, and as a result decided start his own business.

Emotions and feelings drive you throughout the entire lifetime of your business. One day you feel great because you signed on a new recruit or you made a big sale, and another day you feel down because your sales are down and everyone told you no that day. These are the ups and downs of the business. It isn't any different from any other aspect of our lives. We all experience the roller coaster called life. The same way we manage our emotions on a day-to-day basis is the same way we must manage our emotions in our business. Being able to manage your emotions can lead you to a tremendous amount of success because you will no longer be a slave to them.

Notice that it wasn't said that you need to control your emotions here; it was said that you should manage them. You cannot control your emotions. These feelings just happen and they fall over you like a spirit and there is nothing that you can do about them other than learn how to manage them. But how do you do that?

Managing your emotions is all about making firm decisions on what you will allow to play in your mind. Your mind is like a playground, and you have to be careful what you allow to play there. You have control over your thoughts and your thoughts control your emotions, so if you can control your thoughts successfully, then you can manage your emotions.

If you don't learn to manage your emotions, then your emotions will control you and you do not want that to happen. This business will take you on a bumpy ride, and you have to be prepared. You will make big money some months and then others you may not, and you will wonder if a trend of momentum will last. You will build relationships with people and they will end up quitting on you, and you will wonder what's going on. This is all normal, so be prepared.

Your belief systems will assist you in pushing through tough times. A positive expectancy and positive beliefs will pull you through. Ask yourself when things go wrong, what do you normally do? Do you get depressed and stay down for days or do you jump up and count it all as joy because of the lessons you've learned? We hope it's the latter. Here are some key ways to manage the emotional aspects of network marketing:

1. **When sales are down:** Do you believe that they will be down forever or is this just a season? Do you believe that activity will pick up? Are you encouraging your team and reaching out to people you know to generate sales? What is your outlook for the future? Have you created plans to ensure things pick up and keep moving? When sales are down you must keep pushing forward in full belief that it is a season and things will get better. You cannot succumb to feelings of defeat. You must keep a positive attitude and most importantly, you must never communicate fear and trepidation to your organization. Even if you are internally afraid, externally you have to project the opposite. You must keep the eye of the Tiger at all times. Then work double-time to get things moving again. Use promotions and contests to help stimulate sales. Promote events and activities to your new people and watch them soar. There is no better way to get out of a sales slump than to sign some new people to your organization. They will help you get back on track emotionally.

2. **When Recruiting is slow or down:** You have to ask yourself the same questions as before? Do you

believe they will be down forever? Do you think that they will pick up? What are you doing to fix it?

In the Bible, in 1 Corinthians 13:4-13, you learn what love is and learning that verse can change your entire business around because it will allow you to manage aspects of your business that you thought you didn't have any control over. It teaches you about enduring all things, believing all things and having hope in all things. Understanding these things are a must to be able to effectively manage your emotions.

When you learn "to love" the action word, you will concern yourself more with giving than receiving. You will view your role as essential in the lives of the people you touch because you will view what you offer as a part of loving or sharing. You will also learn to give and let go. Similar to what we described previously in Chapter Two, it will be easy for you to let go because of your positive expectancy.

A good book that can help you manage your emotions and maneuver in the network marketing jungle is Robert Greene's *48 Laws of Power* and it is a great resource to use not only in life but especially in this industry because as you move up your compensation plan, you will begin to develop a certain level of respect and trust and power. As such, remaining emotionally balanced not just something you want to improve; it is absolutely a must.

Life Lesson

"We have to do the best we can. This is our sacred
human responsibility."

Author: Albert Einstein

Chapter 7

Master the Fundamentals –
Selling, Recruiting, and Training

This book is about increase. It is about going to the next level, which means growth. Growth cannot happen if you do not master the fundamentals of network marketing. I like to break down the fundamentals into three basic areas: Selling, Recruiting and Training. I always tell people that if these three areas in sync, you will have a successful and balanced organization. However, if you're good at one thing and not the others, your organization will be unbalanced. For example, if you're good at sales, but not at recruiting, you will have an organization that basically consists of you and maybe a few other people and you will have high sales. You can make some money, but you will not move up the compensation plan because you must build a team to do that. Or if you're good at recruiting and not good at sales, then you will have an organization that may have a good amount of people, but your volume production will end up being low. A smaller team can out-produce a larger team in sales because the smaller team has mastered the fundamentals of selling. And you will never perfect the art of selling or recruiting without training. Therefore, it is important to spend an adequate amount of time making sure your organization is balanced and that each person who comes through your group understands how to sell, recruit and train.

Mastering the Art of Selling

Many reps come into this business with reluctance because they believe that they're just not good at selling. Network marketing does not require you to sell an overwhelming amount of product or services. If you look at most compensation plans, the monthly requirements for active status is less than $200 in sales production. Most individuals can satisfy this requirement by becoming their own customer of the product they're representing. One of the key strategies for getting to the next level is ensuring that everyone on your team is their own first customer. Doing this will help you in several ways: first, it will help your team members remain active each month, and second, it will help everyone become a better salesperson.

Products will sell themselves when you're using them. Interestingly enough, your product cannot just jump out of the bag and spread itself onto or into someone's body, but if you're using the product and you have radiant skin or recently lost a lot of weight or your energy level has gone through the roof, people will be able to see this and will begin to ask questions like "What are you doing? ", "You smell great. What are you wearing?" or "How do you have so much energy?" These types of questions help you to sell your product and help you become a good salesperson. Even the person who claims they're not a salesperson will have success when they become a user of the product.

Getting to the next level in your business will require you and your entire team to master the art of selling. Therefore, each and every month, you will want to cover as many aspects of selling as possible, and be creative while you're doing it. Here are some suggestions for generating sales:

1. **Host Your Own Event** – If you're a part of a party plan company, you can host your own party. Even if you're not a part of a party plan company, you can host your own event in your home to invite people to come over to sample your product or service. This is a great way to generate sales, as people in general enjoy trying products before they buy them.

2. **Host Your Own Team Event** – You can come together as a team and host a big event where everyone can invite their guests or past hostesses to come out and sample and buy products from your company. This is a great way to increase or generate group sales.

3. **Contact Your Warm Market** – Contact all the people on your warm market list to place orders or re-orders. If you're in the midst of moving up your plan, you can ask them to do you a favor to help you out. Most people respond positively to assisting you with your promotion goals, or to simply doing you a favor.

4. **Catalog Sales** – If your company has product catalogs, you want to get that catalog into the hands of everyone you know. You can have your friends and family host catalog parties for you, where they can gather orders for you and you can reward them for doing it.

5. **Vending or Tabling Events** – These are events in which you can purchase a table or booth and set up a display your product for sales or demonstrations (if your company allows this). Some companies allow you to set up vending tables for demonstration only, while others allow you to sell product as well. Either way, these often provide great ways to generate sales and leads for the business. These events are normally fee-based and

can be expensive. The best way to determine if an event is worthwhile for you is to look at the cost per attendee ratio (basically take the cost of the event and divide it by the number of projected attendees). This essentially gives you the cost per lead and if the ratio is high then it's probably not worth it, but if the ratio is low then it's a good idea to work the event.

6. **Craft Fairs and Flea Markets** – Craft fairs are great places to set up tables and sell product. However flea markets are a little different. Most flea market attendees are looking for bargain items at bargain prices and product distributed via network marketing is not normally discounted. While you will generate sales and leads at a flea market, it is not always the best source for generating sales.

7. **Business to Business** – It is always a good idea to seek sales with businesses that have a need for the product that you sell. If you sell items that are good for new homeowners, realtors would make a good target market for your items, as they could purchase your items as gifts for new homeowners or they can lead you to this group. When seeking out B2B sales, it's always a good idea to narrow your focus to the type of business that will meet the criteria as an entity that has a demand for what you sell.

8. **Door-to-Door** – When seeking to go to the next level, it is always a good idea to execute all types of sales activity. Selling door-to-door is probably the least attractive and scares most people in this business; however, it is a great way to get your neighbors and the entire community to know about your products.

9. **Fundraisers** – If your company allows you to do fundraisers, then presenting the option of using your product as a fundraiser is a great way to

generate high sales volume. You can donate a portion of your personal commission to an organization as a way to get them to sell your product or service, or you can donate your entire commission. Some direct sales companies have this option already built in and all the collateral material you will need to do fundraisers.

It is clear that you should think outside of the box. Always look for new and creative ways to generate sales for your business. As you can see from the list above there are clearly a lot of ways to generate sales. The secret to becoming a master at selling is to focus on what the customer wants and needs, not your own. To become a master seller, you must set yourself up with a strategy for success. Your sales success strategy may look like something like this:

1. First you will identify your **Who?** Who will you approach about your business? You might want to target a particular group and this will become your niche.
2. Then you will formulate your **How?** How will you introduce yourself to these people to approach them about your product or business?
3. **What?** What need or desire will you satisfy with your product or service? What is it about your product or service that you know your potential customers can't live without? What will you say to them? What will you wear? What will your first impression say about you? What objections will they have and how will you overcome them?
4. **When?** When do you plan to close the deal? When are you going to follow-up? When will you ask for re-orders?

A good sale begins days and sometimes weeks in advance. Preparation is key. Knowing what to say and how to respond to rejections are essential. Identifying who you want to target is important as well. Being equipped with all the collateral material and product that you may need is also important, especially in the network marketing industry.

Selling is not about you, even though you have a lot to do with it. I know that sounds like a paradox, and in many ways it is, because while you do not have any control over the way someone responds to you, what you can control is the way you respond to them. You can also do certain things to make sure your customers always have a positive response to you. For example, dressing professionally, always being well-groomed, and having "The Look" plays a part in generating sales. You don't have to be a Miss America, but presenting yourself as if you were in the running won't hurt. When you want to Quantum Leap, you might want to change your look, and when you get ready to make another Quantum Leap, change it again. This will help you get in the zone. To get to the top, you want to get in and stay in the zone.

Masters of selling practice, practice, practice. They practice what to say and how to say it; they review their sales and understand what works and what doesn't. There are hundreds of places and resources dedicated to the art of selling. I would encourage every network marketer to gain some of that knowledge and to put it to use on a daily basis. Great selling doesn't happen overnight, but once you practice over a period of time, you will become a master of your trade.

Master the Art of Recruiting

Big income is made in networking marketing from recruiting or sharing the opportunity. Recruiting more people, who will in turn sell more (and recruit more people), propels Quantum Leaping.

J. Paul Getty said that he would rather have 1% of the efforts of 100 people versus 100% of his own efforts. That is called leverage. Traditional business owners often have a problem understanding this concept; however network marketers understand it clearly. If you own a restaurant and you're the person who opens and closes the restaurant, what happens to you and your business on days when you get sick? Well, network marketing's answer to that question is on the day you get sick, you can rest because you will have a network of others who will support you while they in turn support themselves, and that's what leverage is all about.

Recruiting results in new people coming into your organization. Having new people flow through your team is good because, first and foremost, it will ensure that you have an organization in months ahead. If you were to do an analysis of your organization right now, I could pretty much guarantee that your current sales are being generated by those that are tried and true (your diehard business builders) and those people that have just come into your organization over the past 90 days. Now imagine what your sales would look like if you didn't have any new people sign on over the past three to six months? This would not be a pretty sight. And your sales would be dismal. Your organization needs the excitement and energy that new people bring. There is nothing like having a new person come onto your team who is excited. The energy that a new person carries can re-ignite some of the older folks on your team, and the sales and referrals a new person brings also represents how your organization will continue to expand and grow.

Recruiting vs Prospecting

Be aware that there is a difference between **Recruiting** and **Prospecting**. Signing on or enrolling a new recruit is Recruiting and it is the result of Prospecting, which means exploring, looking for or interviewing the right candidate. In this industry, people do not recruit a lot of people because they don't spend enough time looking for them or prospecting. The key to becoming a master recruiter is to spend more time prospecting, or mining for gold.

You're looking for quality people. I can remember when I was looking to get to the next level in my business, I wrote down on a piece of paper exactly the type of person I was looking for. That paper read something like this: *I am looking for like-minded business women just like me, people who want to go all the way to the top."* I kept that piece of paper in my wallet and took it with me everywhere I went and read it often throughout the day, and those were exactly the type of people I began to attract.

A quality prospect is someone who will give the time, money and commitment necessary to grow their business. They must want to build a business, and they must have the resources and skills necessary to do so. There is no getting around this fact. An unemployed person is not necessarily a quality prospect, because while they may have a lot time, they most likely do not have a lot of money. The old cliché is correct: it takes money to make money. And while a person doesn't have to have a ton of money to be successful in this industry, it does require a certain amount of resources. A quality prospect is also available. That is not to say they aren't busy; busy people actually make great consultants because they know how to get things done with a small amount of time. However, if a person doesn't have time to work his/her business, then that's not a good person for your team. A quality prospect is also committed to the business and to the team. They show up and they move up. They have strong reasons for being committed and their whys are big. Once again, time, money and commitment are three strong characteristics that you should look for in prospects to make your job of building a large network of distributors a lot easier. These distributors will begin to duplicate themselves, and you will end up with a large organization of quality prospects versus having the opposite occur.

Networkers could learn a lesson or two from professional recruiters in Corporate America. When someone from the Human Resources department of a major corporation is looking for a candidate to fill a position, he/she has a listing of required skills that are necessary to perform the job according to the job description, and this ensures that they make the "right" match. In the network marketing industry we don't always seek out quality prospects; we look for anyone who can breathe and that is not necessarily the best way to build your business. If you want a network of individuals who can duplicate your success, then you're looking for a particular type of person who will fit a certain requirement to do the things that you do. Therefore, it is a good idea to list out the kinds of skills you would want your prospects to have. For example, you might search for individuals with:

- Money to be able to finance their investment
- Great Presentation Skills
- A Good Personality

- A Detail-Oriented style
- The ability to Multi-task
- Good Follow-up skills
- Dependability
- A Job
- Credibility and Integrity

These are just some of the qualities you might look for. But it is up to you to decide the type of individuals you want to work with and once you have this decided, you want to begin to think about all the people you know who have these qualities. The names that you come up with when you think about these skills and traits are those that you want to contact first to share with them your business opportunity.

Developing a hit list of people to contact when you begin your business is great. You want to make sure you've contacted all those people on that list and when you're seeking to go to the next level, if those folks on the list have not yet become a part of your business, you might want to give them another call because timing is everything. The first time you called may not have been good for them, but this time may be better. And if it is still not a good time for them to participate in the business with you, then your job is to ask for referrals.

Prospecting individuals to participate in your business is a process. You have to take prospective distributors through a series of steps before they can make a decision regarding whether or not they will want to become a part of your organization. Even though it happens, it is rare that a person who is first introduced to your opportunity immediately decides to jump on board. Beware of people who make these kinds of quick decisions because while you can get excited by the idea of signing on a new recruit, if this person does not produce, you will end up disappointed.

Just like with selling, good prospecting begins with good preparation. If you want to have a good day of meeting new people, you must be prepared to meet them. You should prepare yourself with company materials to share and possibly product as well. Most network marketing companies offer a wide variety of collateral material for use when prospecting. These items could include brochures, CD's, product samples, etc., that you should always carry with you because prospects are everywhere. Prospects are in the grocery store, the library, the park, the laundry mat, the shopping mall, the bank, anywhere you can think of. Everywhere you go, there are prospects, or people that you may run into that fit the description of the kind of person you're looking to partner with in your business. So make sure you're always prepared.

Once you have prospects in your pipeline, begin working on closing them or recruiting them into your organization. The best ways to close a prospect is by picking up the phone and inviting them to participate in a future event. These events could be upcoming opportunity meetings, three-way calls, sizzle or opportunity calls or 1:1 presentations, etc. The key is to make sure the prospect has had multiple impressions of the business opportunity before they sign up.

Close more prospects by picking up the phone

In this day and age when e-mail rules, we often tend to use it as something we can hide behind. Reps say things like, "I sent them an e-mail," or "I put a prospect package in the mail, but they haven't responded." Then I always say,

"Well, did you call?" There is nothing like making a live contact with a prospect. Live contacts build relationships. Live contacts close deals.

When calling a prospect it is important to keep control of the conversation. Normally when you dial someone's number you should not ask to speak with them. If you say, "Hello may I speak to Susan?", this will not be as effective as if you were to say, "Hi. Susan." In the first scenario, it is clear you do not know Susan, or you would have recognized her voice. In the second scenario, it is implied that you and Susan are already good friends. And she will answer the phone wondering why you know who she is and why she doesn't recognize you. She may even feel guilty for not recognizing your voice. Whatever the case may be, you will be on your way. Ask the prospect lots of questions. Interview them (Remember, you're representing the H.R. department of your company and you're looking for someone with the right fit). Ask questions like:

1. So how did you hear about the company?
2. What do you currently do?
3. How much are you willing to invest in a business?
4. How much time are you willing to dedicate?

Your response is always positive and you're going to say things like "Great. We're looking for people like you." You always want to control the conversation and not let it turn into an interview of you. Always make sure you have a two-minute speech ready that details what you do and how you do it. Continue to interview the prospect and let them know what the next steps are. To close the deal, ask questions like:

1. So how does this sound to you? (You listen and prepare yourself to overcome objections)
2. Are you ready to get started now?
3. When will you be ready to get started?

These types of questions will help you get a commitment and get prospects started in the business right away. Practice will help you to become a master at recruiting. Study interviewing books and review strategies on overcoming objections to become better at this. These resources are everywhere. Seek them out and use them.

At the end of the day, mastering the art of selling and recruiting comes down to understanding people. It's all about your people skills and understanding different personality types. Once you're able to do this, you will be able to relate to people on all different levels and from all different backgrounds. This will help you build a solid business. Not all of the relationships will be long-lasting, but they will be memorable.

There have been several books that have been written to help you understand people and I'd like to encourage you to read them. A good one is called the *"Art of Speed Reading People: How to Size People Up and Speak Their Language"* by Paul D. Tieger and Barbara Barron-Tieger. In this business, you want to be able to size a person up as fast as possible and quickly begin to speak their language, because the way to get what you want is to know what others want. This will not only allow you to sell more products and recruit more people, it will also allow you to help your team members move up in the organization.

People love it when you can relate to them. To relate to people they must be able to hear you, and they won't comprehend a word you're saying if you're not speaking in their native tongue. This is the reason why one person can give the exact same message to three people, but each will hear it in their own way and every person will hear different things.

All masters in the network marketing industry have mastered the language of different personality types to be able to Quantum Leap. They not only mastered it, they taught the skill to the leaders in their organization. And once they conquered this skill, their language began to change with different people they met. They use these skills to become an expert at getting people to come to events, getting people to come into the business, getting people to buy product, getting people to move up the compensation plan and more!

There are a lot of different personality types, but I like to roll them into four basic categories: The Good-Timers, The Plain Janes/Joes, The Mother Theresa's and Pope Johns, and the Movers and Shakers.

The Good-Timers love to have a lot of fun. They tend to be flamboyant dressers, wear loud and bright colors and are amused by music and parties. They also tend to be late to everything and can be unreliable.

The Plain Janes/Joes love everything to be simple. They like to see the world in black or white. They're detailed-oriented. They're always prompt and studious. However, they can be a little uptight and overly detailed. They can also be boring and have a low tolerance when things aren't perfect.

The Mother Theresa's and Pope Johns are those who just want to help everyone and save the world. They're very nurturing. And will do pretty much anything you ask of them. But they're often helpful to a fault because they put the needs of others before their own.

The Mover's and Shakers are those folks who are happening. They want to get things going and fast, and they want to make money right now. They tend to make people feel uncomfortable with their swiftness and overwhelming desire to succeed.

Once you know the characteristics of these four personality types, you will be able to size people up quickly and cater your language and presentation to fit their needs. They will hear you and understand you. Let me encourage you to become a student of the personality types by reading books on this subject. This will change your business overnight.

Online Prospecting

The Internet has become a haven for people looking for business opportunities. You can find thousands of good leads for your business online. With the right online marketing tools, you can certainly have success. There are several ways to prospect online. Let's examine a few:

1. **Search Engine Ads** – There are a lot of big search engine companies online, including AOL, Google and Yahoo. For a fee that is calculated based on the number of clicks to your website, you can set up an ad online and whenever someone searches for the keywords that you have bid on, your website will pop up and the individual will have the option to click on your website. Depending on the number of

keywords you bid on this could be as expensive or inexpensive as you choose. A word to the wise: Don't bid on keywords that are too broad, as they will attract those who are not interested in your particular business. It will cause a lot of unfruitful clicks to your web page. Stick to the basics when it comes to online advertising.

2. **Work from Home Web Pages** – You can set up websites with a lot of content for people interested in working from home. On these web pages, you can advertise your own business opportunity, thus providing content and a potential career for those who find your site.

3. **Yahoo Groups** – You can create a Yahoo group that is open to the public regarding your business opportunity and invite those who are interested in learning more to join your group. Once they ask to join and you accept them, you can begin to have dialogs about your particular business.

4. **MySpace.com** - This is a new and popular place for people to find other people who have similar interests. It is a great way to build a network of people just like you. Just be careful with this one because it can be used for some other things that are not business-related.

5. **Online Classifieds** – There are several websites, such as those for Work-at-Home Moms, dedicated to women seeking employment from home. These are excellent sites to place classified ads. The only downside is that you must be diligent and thorough in your follow-up for these sites. People who go to these sites often request information from more than one home-based business so be prepared to answer some key questions so they can compare opportunities.

Using Technology to Quantum Leap

This is a new day and age for network marketers. The Internet has literally changed the way this business is done. Prospects now have the opportunity to do extensive online research into a company before they decide to join. The Internet is also bringing people closer who were normally miles apart. With that being said, let's talk about how to add technology to the mix to make your Quantum Leap.

1. **Video Email and Streaming Video** – Remember that wacky animated family who lived a crazy life in space called "The Jetsons"? While we have not developed space cars, we do now have video phones and video email. Video email and the ability to stream video over the Internet will allow independent distributors to host live webinars or web seminars, and conduct live business presentations. Video email can also be used for training purposes. Imagine the possibilities. Not only will you be able to send an email, you'll be able to broadcast your message live to your team or broadcast a sizzle call to prospects. This is exciting technology that will certainly help take your business to a higher level.

2. **PDAs , Smartphones and Pocket PCs** – There are no more reasons for anyone to ever miss a call or an email as a result of PDAs, Smartphones and Pocket PCs. A PDA is a personal data assistant and Palm One has cornered this market with its Palm Pilot. These devices allow you to do a broad range of activities that are attractive to the person on the go. Traveling with a laptop is almost no longer necessary now that these items have been invented. Blackberry ™ perfected push-through email technology allowing your emails to flow directly from your email address to your cell phone. For a

network marketer this means you can respond quickly to emails, follow up with prospects more easily, and stay on the pulse of your business.

3. **Yahoo Groups** – Creating a Yahoo Group allows for free message boarding for your team and team members. If someone has a question or concern, they can get their questions answered quickly by posting a message to these boards. This is a free service provided by Yahoo.com

4. **Microsoft Outlook** – Outlook is a great tool to use for managing your communications. It is great for managing and filing emails in folders, making them easier to find and allowing you to manage your contacts, tasks, and calendar relatively easily. Outlook sends you event reminders and allows you to prioritize your tasks and events.

5. **E-Cards** – E-cards now make it easy for you to stay in virtual contact with your prospects and customers. You can send an e-card for pretty much any and every occasion. You can also customize them to fit your needs.

6. **Birthday Reminders** – Several programs and software packages now automate birthday reminders, allowing you to remember your consultants', customers' and prospects' birthdays so you can stay in good favor and build great relationships with them.

7. **Evite.com** – An online invitation program that allows you to virtually invite customers and prospects to events. What is so awesome about this program is that you can manage the guest list responses and view those who opened their invitations vs. those who did not. It's a great tool.

8. **Plaxo.com** - Plaxo helps you manage your rolodex. It is powerful because it is an online business card system.

Technology has changed the way so many people do business. And while it is more efficient, it does nothing to build a good quality relationship. That comes from face-to-face interaction with people. Therefore, use technology to enhance your business and help it run more efficiently, but use your mouth to sustain it and talk to people so you can truly get to know them.

Training is Key

Training for a new recruit begins the minute you open your mouth and begin to speak about the business. Your first impression is important because it lays the ground rules for how your new recruit will work his/her own business. It is vital that you get a new person started on the right foot. If you want your business to run like a well-oiled machine, you will want your training system to cover three primary areas: Getting started, advanced training and leadership training. You want to be able to separate your team in these three areas so you're always providing training, motivation and inspiration to meet their needs at every level of advancement and growth.

For you to Quantum Leap to the next level, it is essential that you foster an environment in which your recruits understand the journey they have embarked on. They need to understand that while this doesn't look or feel like a traditional business, a network marketer will need to make most of the same investments that a traditional business owner must make. The primary reason so many networkers move on to become successful women and men in traditional businesses is that they are able to pick up all of the required skills of entrepreneurship through network marketing.

Let your new people know they're in business and they must act accordingly. They must make commitments to their businesses or they will not see their business grow. Your organization depends on the growth of your new recruits. New people must move from being new to being seasoned, and from being seasoned to being on top. Your training systems should foster an environment that will sustain and train them at each level.

"Getting Started" systems should be put in place for new recruits so they can get started in the business in a simple but systematic way. This system should be easily duplicated and simple enough for a young child to follow. Most people get off track when they attempt to put together highly complicated plans and strategies for getting a new person started. The new recruit can become overwhelmed and feel that he/she will never have success. Once a recruit become discouraged, you can basically forget about him/her. Don't even think that this person will ever get started again because he/she won't. Sometimes it happens, but more often than not, it doesn't.

Your "Getting Started" training system should be set up so it becomes a building block system for promotions and growth. In other words, if your getting started system is solid, it can be done over and over again and will produce volume, promotions and should result in getting you to the next level. Make sure your people know the difference between Production activity vs. Non-Production activity. Production activity is all actions that lead to volume or production and include things like sales calls, opportunity meetings and presentations, 1:1 meetings with potential new recruits, parties, book or catalog sales, and events.

Here are some keys to a good getting started system:

1. It consists primarily of volume-related activities. If your system is followed to the letter, new recruits are guaranteed to earn a certain level of income as well as move up a few levels in their marketing plan.

2. It should be a turnkey system. This means that anyone should be able to pick up your system from any part of the country and duplicate the assignments because the system is ready to roll, especially for those interested in rolling with it. You must know that everyone is not going to want to participate at the same level and as such your system should have a landing place for these individuals as well so they don't feel left out.

3. Your system shouldn't be long or complicated. This will only confuse the new recruit. Keep your getting started or quick start programs simple.

4. It should teach your recruits how to get their investments back as fast as possible. When people put out money for a business, they do so with the full expectation that they will get their money back and then some, and you will want to show them the steps necessary to do this.

5. Your system should teach the new rep to become a product of the product or user of the product or service.

6. Right away, you should be showing your recruits business building techniques, like how to secure and build a customer base.

7. Your program should also include some basic training in areas that will help your recruits understand the business.

Advanced training is the next level of training to be incorporated into your system. In this training you want to begin to train your up-and-coming leaders on the following points:

- How to effectively present the business
- How to conduct business opportunity meetings. (These presentations will be different based on the company. Some companies go for a more rah-rah sales type meeting, while others go for a more business-like presentation. Either way, these presentations should all include music, company facts, and lots of emotion, testimonies and recognition, along with a quick training at the end)
- How to effectively communicate to their teams (using the information from understanding personalities)
- How to balance moving into leadership and keeping up their personal sales and recruiting production

Leadership training is an important aspect of your system, as it is the train the trainers portion of your system. At this level, you teach your new leaders how to do what you do. You might want to include:

- How to conduct leadership trainings
- How to establish reporting systems
- How to keep up-and-coming leaders motivated and inspired
- How to stay on a path of continuous self-improvement and personal development

As a leader of leaders, your training will come from industry experts. Your training will come from the folks who have done things that you haven't done yet. You will have to reach out to people in the industry to assist you in your own personal training and development. It is always a good idea to get outside help to keep your business moving and growing in the right direction. As a leader of leaders you will want to learn from the masters. Seek out these people and always continue to grow professionally. This will keep you in the mode of always reaching for the next level. You will never know it all, so it's important to keep learning.

Each quarter, pick an area in your business where you can improve and work toward mastering it. The following list shows areas in which you can excel by seeking assistance through books and courses. Mastering these points will help you tremendously in your business.

1. Building Effective Relationships
2. Public Speaking
3. Selling and Sales Techniques
4. Image Consulting
5. Effective Writing and Communication Skills
6. Computer Skills: Word, Excel, Outlook, etc.
7. Organizational Skills
8. Time Management
9. Positive Thinking/Attitudes

10. Emotional Management

11. Becoming a Certified Coach

Staying in a continuous learning phase will not only keep you going in your business, it will keep you at the top of your game. It has been said that people who continuously learn never grow old. Maybe learning is the real fountain of youth, so why not give it a shot. However you look at it, it is a must for network marketing success.

Life Lesson

"Nothing great was ever achieved without enthusiasm."

Author: Ralph Waldo Emerson

Chapter 8

Have High Energy

This business is all about the energy, or the capacity for a physical system (like the human system) to do work. Your business has energy. It has an ability to work. Most people are looking for their business to work in some form or fashion, meaning that they're looking for their business to produce at the level in which they've set for themselves. The energy of your business is a direct reflection of the leader. If you don't have a high level of energy to pump into your business then it's not going to work for you.

Imagine walking into a room where it is dead quiet. What kind of energy does this room possess? Dead energy. Right? Your first thought for that room may be, "Nothing is going on in there." But if you walked into a room where it is lively, people are interacting and having a good time and music is playing, not only will your spirits be lifted when you enter that room, but people who weren't intending to go into that room will be drawn to it because of the positive and lively energy that emanates from it. This is the type of energy you want to have in your business.

You have to have high energy to take your business to the next level. Truth be told, to Quantum Leap, your energy has to be so over the top to the point of it being ridiculous. You must have Anthony Robbins type energy, or Chris Rock type energy. If you get a chance watch these two in action you will notice that their energy is amazing and it is transferable to the people around them. Therefore if you want the people on your team to move, you've got to move.

Energy is a precious commodity. In Chapter Six we noted that you must develop an Amen corner, and this is because certain people, places and things will zap your energy. Some energy stealers you might come across include the TV, the News, Negative People, Sugary Sweets, etc. There are so many things out there that steal our energy, we have to constantly take action to keep our energy levels high.

Hey, honestly do you think a person will want to come to a meeting or take their time to hear a person speak if that person is boring and tired and has no energy. No! That's why you have to have high energy for your Quantum Leap.

Energy Boosters:
- Green Drink – When I was on the path to the next level, drinking a good green energy drink helped me tremendously. Green drinks come primarily in a powdered format and they provide a high dosage of green vegetables, which help to balance the body. I thought I would hate it, but I loved it.
- Vitamins – A good multi-vitamin can give you a major push when you're on a path to success. There is no way we can get all we need with our diets, so we must supplement.
- Exercise – The endorphins will kick in when you exercise and they will give you a boost that will put you into overdrive.
- Adequate Sleep – Sleep is something that you will treasure AFTER you Quantum Leap, but while you're in the process of going to the next level, your

excitement and energy will be so high, your mind may not allow you to sleep. This is not necessarily a bad thing; just be sure to get adequate sleep so your body continues to operate at an optimal level.

- Massages – Get a good massage once a month. I would encourage anyone to add this to your wellness plan. This will give you a tremendous amount of energy.
- Dancing – Get up and dance like nobody's watching and see how your energy level changes.
- Smiling – Just smile right now and see how your entire attitude shifts. Go ahead smile. I dare you.
- Singing – You don't have to be in the shower; sing anywhere. Just sing your favorite song, especially if it alters your mood.
- Listening to upbeat music – This is so important. Go to iTunes.com and find your favorite hits. Burn them onto a CD and name it "My Songs." Then take it with you wherever you go to help lift your spirits.

Positive Energy – Love

My business changed significantly when I began to learn to love, the action word. I began to love everything and everybody for who they were. I began to love their so-called faults and flaws because I understood that this is what makes them uniquely who they are. I accepted those things that I could not change and I began to love everything. When orders came on time, I loved it. When they didn't, I learned to love that too because I knew there was a lesson to be learned.

I began to love all the people. I loved those who were responsive and those who were not. I loved those who did well and those who didn't. It didn't matter. I connected on a higher level to God and saw the beauty in it all. That positive energy began to wrap its arms around the organization and shelter it. When I learned to love, I became better at selling. When I learned to love, I became better at recruiting. The energy of love sent people my way and we began to receive God's favor.

Positive Energy – Forgiveness – Learn to forgive people who say they're going to come to a meeting and don't show. Learn to forgive people who say they're going to sign up and then don't. To remain positive and sane in this business, you must learn to forgive those who do not do the things they said they would do. Sometimes people have good intentions and life gets in the way. Being able to forgive is positive.

Protect your energy at all costs. Keep it shielded from the energy stealers. We have a lot of them in the world, they're called TV, DVDs, News, Newspapers, Trash Magazines, etc. They surround us every day and work hard to bring us down. Stay clear of these things and stay positive; this will keep your energy levels high and you will float, better yet, fly.

Life Lesson

"It's always too soon to quit"

Author: Norman Vincent Peale

Chapter 9

Never Give Up

You must be unstoppable to Quantum Leap. You must know with every essence of your being that "Quitters Never Win and Winners Never Quit." That's the bottom line. You have to come to the table with amazing strength and burning desire. Your desire has to be so hot that people can look at you and see the steam rising from your brow. You have to possess the look. It will show in your eyes.

When you want something bad enough nothing will keep you from it. Everyone can remember a time in their life when they pursued something with so much passion, they wondered in amazement how they got the energy or strength to make it happen. It could have been losing weight for an event, planning a huge wedding, giving birth or getting a graduate degree. Whatever it is, when your desire is strong, nothing can stop you. You will be able to tear down walls you never thought or imaged you could.

Pursuing something important to you begins with believing in yourself and your ability to do the things that you set out to do. When you look over your life, what do you see? Do you see a lot of ideas and projects that you started but never finished? Do you see Ralph Cramden of the old hit show "The Honeymooners"? Remember Ralph? He was the one who always had the great ideas, but never had the fortitude to stick it out with any of them or didn't think a project out before diving in headfirst and ending up landing flat on his stomach.

Maybe this is you. And maybe this is the reason your family and friends run every time they see you. They're scared and trying to figure out what you're into next because in their minds you're always into something. If this is the case, you can clearly see why your family and friends are sick and tired of you making "excuses" about why something did or did not work. At the end of the day, you will discover that you had a good opportunity but you quit before you could have a chance to experience success.

At the end of the day, with network marketing you have to pick a horse and ride it. You must ride it all the way to the finish line. This industry is filled with dream seekers who hop from one opportunity to the next, but to be successful, you must pick one. Most network marketing companies will not allow you to reach a certain level of leadership and still have a relationship with another company. They know that you cannot serve two masters. So, you must pick one and have the stick-to-it-ness to stay for the cross-country trip.

Two Network Marketing representatives, one with the ID number 123 and one with the ID number 124, clearly came into the business together. About five years after starting, consultant 123 ran into 124. Consultant 123 was in town for a training session and was free from Corporate America and living her dreams. She invited the now former consultant 124 to come to the meeting. Consultant number 124 couldn't make the meeting though because she had to go to her part-time job at Carmax. How sad a story is that? Consultant 123 confessed that she was where she was, which was at the top of her company, because she had not quit. The other consultant had given up and as a result, she was in the same condition that she was before. And now instead of working a business that could potentially set her free, she was working part-time and had no-time for her. What a powerful argument for never giving up.

For some people, their success is going to come fast and furious, while for others it is going to progress like molasses rolling uphill – extremely slow. But success is destined for all who are determined to finish the race. Runners race to the finish line. This is what we all must do with our businesses. I can remember running a half marathon many years ago. I was almost at the end, and I was tired and my body ached all over. The sweat on my skin was literally turning into salt crystals. But I kept going, even if I had to walk a little bit, I kept going because I knew beyond a shadow of a doubt that eventually I would cross the finish line and would be a winner because I did not quit. This is what network marketers must do to go to the next level; they must realize that they have to go all the way. And they understand that the race is not given to the swift, but to those who endures it to the end.

Life Lesson

"To laugh often and love much; to win the respect
of intelligent persons and the affection of children,
to earn the approbation of honest critics; to
appreciate beauty; to give of one's self, to leave the
world a bit better, whether by a healthy child, a
garden patch or a redeemed social condition; to
have played and laughed with enthusiasm and
sung with exultation; to know even one life has
breathed easier because you have lived — that is to
have succeeded."

Author: Ralph Waldo Emerson

Chapter 10

You've Made It, Now What?

You've made it to the top of your Network Marketing business, good for you! Now what? I can remember reaching the top position in my company's compensation plan just like it was yesterday. It was a major event. I received so many e-mails, kudos and kind messages, I was boiling over with happiness. But I must say that the next week, I was down and out wondering where I was supposed to go from here. If you've ever planned a wedding or major event, or even had a baby, you understand the feelings that occur once the event is over. In pregnancy, they call it postpartum depression. Well, I guess I had what you could call post-promotion syndrome. It is the feelings you get once you've promoted and all the excitement wears off. No one prepares you for this, but it happens. And because it does, I must offer this advice to those who have made a Quantum Leap.

Develop a Financial Plan

A lot of successful Network Marketers end up broke. How does this happen? How can someone go from earning $50,000 per month to bankruptcy? It happens because they never had a financial plan. They never understood what they needed to do with their money to hold onto it.

In you're working as an independent consultant, you're not considered an employee and taxes are not withdrawn from any commissions that are rendered to you. As a result, if you are not a good steward to your money, you may end up getting into financial trouble. When you are an employee of a company, the employer often provides savings plans like 401k's, and they withhold funds from your income for the federal, state and local governments for tax purposes. However, when you are on your own, no one will do this for you automatically, and you will have to do it for yourself. Additionally, your company from your corporate job may have provided several types of insurance for you at a discounted rate, including life, disability and health insurance and these are things that you will also have to begin to provide for yourself.

These are big shockers for most people who go full-time with their business. They don't realize that they must now begin to operate professionally as any other business would. If nothing else brings you to the reality of this, learning how to manage your finances will. I'd like to offer up some key points toward developing a sound financial plan once you've made a Quantum Leap and especially if you've gone full-time with your business.

1. **Incorporate** – You should incorporate your business from the start. Many Network Marketing companies do not allow you to transfer your business. Therefore, if something were to happen to you, your business would be surrendered to the company. However, if you were incorporated, someone in your family could work your business and continue to receive the residual income from it. It now becomes transferable. This is the most important reason you should incorporate right from

the start. A Limited Liability Corporation (LLC) is one of the most popular forms of corporations today for small businesses. It is relatively easy to form, and it is not necessary for you to pay preparation fees to an attorney to form an LLC on your behalf. Your state website has all the forms you need listed there. Even the name search database is normally included online for you to search the name that you want to use for your LLC. In a few easy steps - choosing a name and filing Articles of Organization (forms available on state web site) - create your LLC Operating Agreement and obtain licensing and permits. If you follow the directions online with your local state government, this can be done in a few hours if you pay to have it expedited. This is a good thing to do.

2. **Get a Good Accountant** – You will need a good accountant to assist you in the management of your funds. You will have taxes to pay on a quarterly basis, and you will have want to have someone knowledgeable to help you set yourself up to maximize your income and limit your tax liabilities.

3. **Open a SEP-IRA** – You will want to begin to save money for yourself the same way you did when you worked for someone else. It is important to set up a Self-Employed Persons–IRA account, which will allow you to save money and receive the same tax benefits you would have received from having a 401k.

4. **Get Health Insurance** – If you're married, and your spouse works, you should be able to get on his/her health insurance plan. You will want to do this right away. You do not want to spend any amount of time without good health insurance. Your health is your wealth and you must take special care to make sure

that you stay up to par physically. If you're single, you will want to find reasonably priced health insurance. www.ehealthinsurance.com can help you find affordable health, dental and vision insurance.

5. **Get Life and Disability Insurance** – It is especially important to get good life insurance if you have children. You will want to have your children well taken care of in the event something unfortunate happens to you. A good life insurance policy is crucial to that process. Take some time out to shop around and determine what is right for you. There are so many types of life insurance policies out there it can be confusing, so do your homework and find something that works and fits in best for you and your lifestyle.

6. **Pay Your Taxes** – Do whatever it takes to pay your taxes quarterly and on time. Make sure you have set up with your accountant a system for you to pay your federal, state and local taxes. Otherwise, at the end of the year you may face harsh tax liabilities and penalties.

7. **Get a Separate Business Account** – You will want to keep the money related to your business separate from the money you use for your personal household budgeting. This will provide clean record keeping for you, especially during tax time.

8. **Set Up a Monthly Budget** – All that money does not belong to you. That is a great mantra to live by when you're a successful business owner. It is so easy to receive a large commission check and think that it's time to go shopping when the bills have not yet been paid. You must pay all your bills and yourself first when setting up your monthly budget. Make sure you include all your incidental expenses in your budget as well. Make sure that your budgeting

system is as accurate and comprehensive as possible. Budgeting and tracking all of your monthly expenses is probably one of the most difficult things you're going to have to learn to do, but you must do it, or you will run into financial woes.

Spend Some Time Working on You

We spend a lot of time working toward success in businesses, but we fail to spend the time necessary working on our own, and sometimes physical, needs. We often neglect our bodies when we're working hard toward success in business. Once you've reached some of your major goals, make time to get the appropriate amount of exercise and rest that your body needs. Take time out to meditate, read or simply Be. Take walks on the beach or in the park and spend some time listening to your thoughts. Treat yourself well. If you would like to a movie or play, do that. Maybe you'd like a massage or to spend a day at a Spa, and you should do that as well. You may have always wanted to take a class to learn how to sew, and this is a great reward for all your hard work too! This is the time to do all those things that you've wanted to do, but never had the time to.

Expand Your Horizons

There may have been something in life that you've always wanted to do but you didn't have the time or money for it. But now you do have time and money, and this is the time to expand your horizons and make those elusive dreams happen. Maybe you wanted to learn to ski or rock climb, or take a cruise or travel to Europe. Maybe you've always wanted to learn another language or a new skill, and now that you've gone to the next level in your business, you should do those things that you've always wanted to do.

Look for New Hills to Climb

First and foremost, you want to look for new hills to climb. You will want to begin to set new goals and standards for yourself so that you can continue to stay in motivated and high-production mode. If there are areas you have not conquered in your business, seek to conquer them. All companies have different production clubs and you should attempt to get into these clubs if you haven't done so before. Doing this will keep you challenged; otherwise, you run the risk of getting bored. Also, you can create your own challenges and goals, such as creating a certain number of new leaders or recruiting a certain number of new people. You have to think of ways to keep yourself excited and plugged in. There are always new things that you can do to keep your business moving in the right direction. Your job is to find those things and do them.

Find Something Else to Do

Find something else to do that is complimentary and noncompetitive to your business. You can do something like write a book or record a CD. These things will generate extra income and create multiple streams of income for you and can be easily done while you work and build your Network Marketing business.

Get a Life

Get a life if you don't have one, or live your life if you do. Many people find that when they're going to the next level in their business, they sometimes tend to neglect the things that matter most. Relationships, family and friends sometimes get neglected when we're running to the top. Once you've achieved your major goal, take some time out to spend quality time with your family and friends. Work on building new relationships if you're single and work on your existing relationship if you're married. There is no sense to getting all of the financial rewards in your business if you don't anyone to share it with.

Start Your Dream Business

Remember when you used to dream about starting your own business? Maybe this is what made you decided to actually start your own Network Marketing business. Well, once you've had a tremendous amount of success in your Network Marketing business, to the time is right for you to consider starting that dream business. There is no better time to do this than once you've reached the top position in your company. This is the time in which you want to chart new courses of action.

Take Your Dream Vacation

Maybe there is someplace you've always wanted to go or something that you've always wanted to do...well, what are you waiting for? You've made your Quantum Leap; now is the time to have some fun and travel to those places you've always wanted to see.

After you've made your Quantum Leap, remember to relax. Enjoy life. Live. You've worked hard and you deserve it.

Epilogue

The Truth About Network Marketing

Network Marketing is the only industry that levels the playing field in America. It is the last standing business that allows anyone who participates the opportunity to earn unlimited income based on his/her own efforts. When you work in direct sales, you get paid and that's the bottom line. What you put in is what you get out. There are no short cuts and no get rich quick schemes. It is an industry in which good honest hard work gets rewarded. Now that is not to say that there are not any companies out there that are "fake" and give the industry a bad name, but the majority of them are real. When you find a reputable company that offers a product or service that you believe in and can also turn around and sell that product to a customer and build a customer base as well as a distribution team, then you've found something that could potentially change your life and the financial history of your family.

A lot of people enter into Network Marketing thinking that immediately they're going to become rich. And this is no surprise in this microwave generation of people seeking now money now. Therefore, when the income doesn't come as fast as they can pop popcorn in the microwave, they are quick to say that it doesn't work. Well, that's incorrect. Network Marketing does work. It especially works for those who do not quit. For those who see it to the finish line, they often find a pot of gold is waiting for them at the end.

Network Marketing is an industry that is also often misunderstood. Many people get involved and think that it's supposed to work like a regular J-O-B and are disappointed when they find that it's not about trading time for money. The industry doesn't work like that. When an individual decides to open up his or her own networking marketing business or franchise, they immediately become the President and CEO of their own business. It's similar to opening up a hamburger joint or any business franchise. You have to work hard in the initial stages of your business in order for you to see a profit. When most businesses submit their business plans to banks, the first 3 years tend to show their income in the red. Usually it is not until around the 4th year of operations that their business begins to show some kind of profit. It's normally around year 4 or 5 that the business begins to pop or begins to show real promise of success. Network Marketing isn't any different. Yet because most people are used to working a 9 to 5 (trading time for money) and are conditioned to getting a paycheck, they can't seem to wrap their arms around the concept of working so many hours to get a small return in the beginning. But this is the reality for most small business owners, which is the primary reason why many businesses fail within the first three years or less. Once a person understands that it takes time to build a regular brick and mortar business then they can understand that the same holds true for Network Marketing. In fact the average person starting out can expect to earn between $300-$500/mo in their first couple of months, however, this is good news considering that the average American family is only $300 extra dollars away from paying their bills on time. That extra money can help a lot of people. *NY Times* best selling author, David Bach wrote in his latest book, *Start Late Finish Rich,* that direct sales is one way that the average American can get the extra $500-$1000 per month that they need to retire rich.

In the preceding pages, I present some of the basic truths about the industry. These truths are meant to shift the mindset of those currently involved in network marketing (as well as those that are not) because in order to Quantum Leap you must have the right mindset and you must understand the intricacies and truths about the business you're in.

Truth #1 – Network Marketing is not a pyramid scheme. The Network Marketing industry is not made up of pyramid schemes. People often believe that the person on top will always be on top and that no one can rise above that person or team. This is not true. Time and time again, new people are signing onto Network Marketing organizations and blowing past current leaders, and as I type this sentence, someone is getting blown past right now.

Nevertheless, people continue to perpetuate this myth. If anyone took the time to do some analysis, they would discover that Corporate America, as well as the United States government, are set up like pyramids. When you look at the organizational structure of most corporations, you will find a CEO/President, and maybe some Sr. Vice Presidents under him and some Vice Presidents under him, and then some Sr. Directors under them and then Directors, then Managers, etc. And what you might notice is that the closer you get to the top, the smaller the number of people, and the closer you get to the bottom, there are more people. Hmmm!!!! Sounds like the shape of a pyramid doesn't it? The most ironic thing about this structure is that, when you are hired by the Corporation, are you hired as the President and CEO? No! You're hired at the bottom of the pyramid, and you're expected to work your way up. But how is that possible when the people at the top are constantly fighting to maintain their positions of power and prestige? How long do you think it would take you to get to the top of your corporation? If you answered "a long time", you're right, and if you answered "never," you're even more right.

Unlike Corporate America, Networking Marketing is the only opportunity that allows you to start at the top. You can get started with most Direct Sales (Network Marketing) companies for less than $500. Where else can you start up a business or franchise with such a small investment and then turn around and work your way to millionaire status? Only in Network Marketing can you do such a thing and that's the beauty of this industry. Like I said before, the playing field is level. This industry doesn't care if you're black, white, fat, tall, or skinny, all that this industry cares about is whether or not you have a passion and desire for success. When you embrace a Network Marketing opportunity with an open mind and a willingness to be coached, you will be transformed!

So what is Network Marketing then? Many ask this question because they don't understand the concept of Direct Selling. Direct Selling is a different form of distributing a product or a service. Traditional distribution methods have failed many companies. A new company develops a product and seeks to get it placed on the shelves of stores throughout the U.S. This can be costly for the company, because even if they were able to get the product placed on the shelves, they still would have to advertise that the product is there. Those advertising dollars and middleman costs virtually disappear when a company decides to distribute their product via word-of-mouth marketing or Direct Sales. And most of those savings are passed on to the independent distributor in the form of commissions.

So many companies today have discovered that this is such a great form of distribution that even more traditional product companies are looking to Direct Sales as a method of distributing their products. Everything you can possibly think of has been and continues to be distributed via Network Marketing, which guarantees that the industry will be around for a long time.

Truth #2 – The real money is in team building. While selling product will earn most independent representatives a healthy commission, one of the truths of network marketing is that you will not make big bucks in any company if you do not build a large organization. Distribution is the name of the game and for an independent representative, your role is to build the largest pool of distributors that you possibly can. And how you build a large team is by finding a handful of key business builders. These key business builders will duplicate your efforts and build large organizations for themselves, which by default will grow your own, and this leads to the next Truth.

Truth #3 – It only takes about five quality business builders to build a large organization. It only takes a handful of people to build a large team and most companies are made up of a few people whose teams drive company sales. Your job as a professional business builder is to find like-minded individuals to help you grow your team. Recruit people in your business who understand network marketing or those who have a good business sense, and they will be your saving grace, your business builders. If you recruit people that don't fall into the quality prospect category, you're only going to frustrate yourself and end up spinning your wheels. You will also send your business spiraling downward because individuals with the wrong mindset or understanding will end up recruiting people that are just like them and that will be the beginning of a faltering and failing organization. This negative trend will also negatively affect your income. Therefore, your goal is to avoid this at all cost and how you do that is by determining ahead of time what a quality prospect means to you and work toward finding them. It's like finding a needle in a haystack. But it is worth the search if it means creating walk-away income for you and your family. And if you don't know what walk-away income is, it is the kind of income that you earn even if you walked away from the business, it's also known as residual income.

Truth #4 – You will have to sort through hundreds of people to find those 5 quality business builders. While it only takes a few quality people to blow out your organization, you will sort through hundreds of people before you find your five or more life-long business builders. This is the reality of the business. Now this sort can take you several months or it may take you several years depending on the amount of work you're willing to do. Always remember that it's up to you. A large part of your success depends on your own efforts.

Truth #5 - You cannot make a lot of money off your family and friends. While it's okay to launch your business by presenting it to your family and friends, you should know that it is not possible to get rich off of them. Your family and friends are also known as your warm market in this industry and the best thing that you can do with folks that fall into this category is make them your customers (if you can do that much with them), and keep moving. Don't get hung up if you cannot get their support. Most of the time, your family and friends will be the last to support you in your business venture, so the best thing you can do is move on from them quickly and ask them for referrals. Always remember that it's not about them, it's about who they know. Your goal is to keep your rolodex growing by constantly asking for referrals, because even though a referral may not be someone you know from your warm market, at least they're not completely cold.

Truth #6 – You will have to talk to people you don't know. Your family and friends are going to run out in about 2 days, or 2 weeks if you're lucky. After you've called everyone you think you know, you're going to have to resort to talking to people you don't know. If you are looking to be successful and make a Quantum Leap, you will have to speak with a lot of people that you do not know. Remember you are sorting through people to find those key business builders who will help you build a dynasty of distributors.

Truth #7 – Network Marketing is a transient business. People will come and people will go, there is no getting around this basic truth. The sooner you thoroughly understand this concept the better off you will be. Network marketing has a high attrition rate and what this means is that people will quit. Your business is like a revolving door. Some will stay for a couple of weeks, some a couple of months, and some a couple of years. Your goal is to make sure that their stay is as life-changing and memorable as possible. It's like being in the hotel business, which is another business in which folks are just passing through. Guests are constantly checking in and checking out, but this doesn't make the owner mad or sad. This makes the owner happy doesn't it? Because as people are checking in, the owner is happy because he knows that his new guests are excited and will spend money in his establishment. He is also happy when the guest checks out because he knows that he has learned something from their visit and now it's time to make room for new people. The hotel owner politely opens the door for the guest to come in and politely opens the door when they leave.

This is the attitude that one must take toward his/her business. You must understand that the business is filled with moments and memories and that your job is to make sure that as long as the new recruit is in your space or on your team, his or her life is forever transformed and blessed and that you have encouraged that person in some way. This is what the real network marketing experience is all about. It is about building relationships like a hotel owner does with his guests to make sure that the recruits and customers keep coming back.

Truth #8 --You will need a lot of Energy to achieve success. In this business you will find that you're in contact with a tremendous number of people. As such, you will notice that people are either energy givers or energy takers. In fact, most are energy takers and you will need a lot of energy to deal with it. Therefore, it is important to get plenty of rest, eat healthy and exercise. These three things represent a power formula for keeping you operating at peak levels. You can also ensure you have optimal energy by adding supplements to your diet regimen. There is no way to get all the vitamins and nutrients we need on a daily basis with the diets of today, so it is vital to your health to take supplements. These will keep you on your feet and you won't be winded and worn out after presentations or weeks and weeks of dealing with people. Imagine yourself presenting at an all-day training session and at the end of the event everyone is asking for photos and autographs. By the end of the day, you are wiped out and then the group decides to invite you out to dinner. That evening, your eyes close before your head can even hit the pillow. You are exhausted. This is where your supplemental support comes in. It will help you to push through times like these so that you wake up the next morning ready to go and do it all over again. And with that being said, a high level of energy is absolutely required and always necessary. It is your job to find out what works for you. Continue to tweak your program until you have the "right" formula to give you all the energy you need to climb to the top of your company's compensation plan.

Truth #9 – You must stay committed and plugged in. Because Network Marketing has one of the highest attrition rates of most industries, you must make sure that your team members stay plugged in to your system. Ninety percent of the people that come into a particular company will quit. Some come back and some are gone forever. If you want to have real success and earn a healthy six-figure income, you will have to stay committed and plugged in to the happenings of your company. Each day of each month is a new opportunity for you to learn and grow, and as such you have to take advantage of every opportunity. If your company has a contest going on, you will want to participate in it. But how will you know about it if you're not plugged in? You must participate in the conference calls, meetings and conferences your company has going on. It is critical to your success.

It never ceases to amaze me how many people miss out on promotions or opportunities to build or increase their income because they weren't plugged in. They have a nonchalant attitude toward their business or they treat it as a hobby. They don't participate in meetings and they don't log on to their computer to read e-mails, and as a result, they have no clue about what is happening in their organization. Then, when they miss out on something important and it costs them commissions, they feel bad and get upset. If they simply tuned in to what had been going on with their company, this never would have happened to them. Don't let this happen to you. Stay plugged in to your system, whatever it may be.

Truth #10– Network Marketing is simple, but not easy. Network marketing is a simple business, but it is not necessarily easy. The work is easy, but dealing with so many people makes it difficult. The paradox is that it is by far probably the easiest hardest work you will ever do.

Part II

Quantum Leap:
How to make a Quantum Leap In
Network Marketing
The Workbook

By

Toni Coleman Brown

Chapter 11

The Message is Clear that You Must Work

More than 10 years ago, I was invited to visit Christian Cultural Center in Brooklyn, also known as CCC. Back then, the church was located on Linden Blvd. There was a line of people waiting in freezing New York weather to get into the church to hear the young pastor A.R. Bernard deliver his message. As people left the church, each person relayed the message that it was worth the wait. So I anxiously waited to get inside to hear this message. Pastor Bernard is known as a teacher pastor. He doesn't merely relay a message of damnation or salvation, he teaches the Bible so you can use it in your life today. On this particular day, he was talking about the miracles that Jesus performed in the Bible. He explained how before each miracle was performed, God gave each of the recipients something to do. The message was clear: God doesn't give you anything without first giving you an assignment to complete.

I learned that day that nothing in life comes easy. You have to work. You have to work hard. If you want to get to the next level in your network marketing business, it's going to take hard work. There are no shortcuts in this industry. If there were, everyone would be wealthy and at the top of the compensation plans. However, if you took a peak inside any network marketing company you will find that only a select few make it to the top. Nevertheless, the beauty of the industry is that anyone who has a burning desire to make it to the top can do just that if they put in the necessary work.

This workbook section is designed to assist those individuals who have a sincere desire to reach the top of their company. It is laid out in a clear, concise manner to help you assess where you are and map out a plan for getting where you want to go. It doesn't matter if you want to get to the top or just make more than you're earning right now. If you complete the work in this workbook, it will help you get there. This workbook was based on the actions steps I took to get to the top of my current compensation plan and triple my income. I know it can do the same for you.

Good luck and congratulations in advance. I would love to hear about your success. Please send your responses to acole225@aol.com

Chapter 12

 **Getting Started**

It doesn't matter where you are, when it comes to making a Quantum Leap in your business, you have to start right there. So you must take an assessment. Are you a brand-new representative just starting out? Or have you been working your business for quite some time and have decided to go to another level. Whatever your position, once you decide to move, you have to go. When you decide that you want to run with the giants or top producers in your company, it is a race to the finish line, and you must keep running until you cross it.

First things first. You want to know where you are currently in relation to where you want to go. Are you in the bottom half or the top half? Whose team are you on? What is your sponsor's title? Are you ahead of your sponsor or behind him/her? Do you need to seek help above him or her? Or do you need to seek help outside the organization? Are you on a winning team? These are some of the things that you must to know. Find out where the resources are for you to get your questions answered and don't be afraid to be a pest. Finding out what you need to know to get ahead is vital to your success. Finding out who you need to talk to is also key. The one thing you don't want to do is take advice from someone who has not had any success in the business. That will put you on the wrong track. So seek out the winners, the top money earners/top producers and spend a healthy amount of time picking their collective brain.

This workbook will provide you with a profile of what a top producer's organization looks like and can help you with the questions you might want to ask a leader in your company. Before you go that far, however, you want to first understand *why* you want to move up in your organization and *what* your vision of the future looks like. Once you have a clear picture of what your future looks like, it can help you fuel your desire to get ahead. So let's begin.

Let's take a look at your organization. It is important for you to assess where you are to be able to understand what the gap is between where you are and where you want to go before you can make a Quantum Leap.

Your Organization:
1. Your Start Date:_____ How long in business? _____
2. How many team members do you currently have?_____
3. How many team leaders or A-players are on your team?_____
4. Do you maximize your income each month by getting paid on your entire team? (Y/N)
5. What's your current title?_____How many titles are there between your current title and the top title in your plan?____
6. How much do you earn each month?_____
7. How much would you like to earn each month?_____

Exercise: Take how much you would like to earn and divide it by the amount that you currently earn. Then take that number and multiply it by your team size. This is the approximate number of team members you will need to produce the income that you're looking for.

(Example: If you want to earn $10,000/mo and you currently earn $1,000/mo, divide $10,000/$1,000 = 10. And if you currently have 100 team members, multiply that by 10 = 1,000. This means that you will need approximately a team size of about 1,000 team members to earn $10,000/mo)

8. What is the target date for your next promotion?_____
9. Why do you want to move up your plan?

_____

_____

_____

10. How will your life change once you reach the top and you're earning the amount of income you desire?

_____

_____

11. What will you do differently than you are doing right now and why?

_____

_____

_____

12. What would stop you from getting what you want and having the life you desire?

Tip: Box Up What You Think Will Stop You and Throw It Out. Nothing Can Stop You From Getting What You Desire.

13. You are currently at the top of the compensation plan and you're making the income you desire. What do you see?

_____

_____

_____

(Take your time to paint the vision for what your life will look like. Make sure you use all five senses, touch, smell, taste, sight, and sounds, to paint this picture. Use extra paper if you need to. Once you have this vision clearly painted, rewrite it on a separate sheet of paper and make copies. Put it all over where you can see it and get to it and read it several times a day. Over time you will find yourself coming closer and closer to making your vision a reality). Congratulations!

Business Vision Statement
What is your vision for your business? What kind of business are you operating? Take some time out to develop your business vision statement.

Example:
I have a team of dedicated and motivated leaders who are consistently moving up in the compensation plan. They're a group of take-charge individuals who know how to get things done. I have grown and nurtured hundreds of

people to the top and each month, they're earning checks with commas in them and lots of zeros. I can confidently work with my personal team, knowing the leaders have duplicated the success of our system.

<u>Now Write Yours:</u>

_____

_____

_____

_____

_____

_____

_____

_____

_____

_____

_____

_____

_____

_____

Profile of a Top Money Earner

So you want to make a Quantum Leap and become a top money earner in your company? One of the keys to becoming a top money earner is having a keen understanding of what a top producing business unit looks like. The reality might be shocking to you. But if you want that kind of income, you're going to have to duplicate the efforts of that organization to duplicate that kind of performance. There is no reason to re-invent the wheel; simply sit down and have a conversation with the top producers or the person who is making the kind of income that you would like to earn.

Here are some things you will want to know:

1. **What are the requirements for reaching the top position in the company?**
   - **Organizational**_____
   - **Personal Production**_____
   - **Team Production**_____
   - **Other**_____

2. **How many people does the Top Money Earner /Producer have on his/her team?**_____

3. How many people has the Top Money-Earner /Producer personally recruited?_____

4. If your plan is a multi-level plan, how many people does the Top Money-Earner/Producer have on his/her levels 1-8 etc.?
   - Level 1_____   Level 4_____
   - Level 2_____   Level 5_____
   - Level 3_____   Level 6_____
   - Level 7_____   Level 8_____

5. What kind of team production does the Top Money Earner produce each month?_____

6. What kind of personal production does the Top Money Earner produce each month?_____

7. What is the minimum number of team members needed to reach the top of your plan?_____

8. How long did it take the Top Producer to reach this rank?_____

9. How many team members does the Top Money Earner bring to Corporate and Team events?_____

10. How many people does the Top Money Earner recruit on a monthly basis?_____ And sell on a monthly basis?_____

Take some time to interview some of the Top Producers in your organization and find out the answers to these questions. Compare their answers to your own and you will begin to discover what you will need to do on a regular basis to get to the top of your compensation plan.

All top producers and top money earners begin this business exactly at the same place you do. They all start at ground zero and work their way to the top. You can do the same if you simply follow their lead and remember that there is no need to re-invent the wheel. Simply duplicate what has already been done.

GOAL SETTING WORKSHEET

GOAL:
TARGET DATE:
WHY?

KEY ACTION STEP: DUE DATE:

KEY ACTION STEP:	DUE DATE:
1.	
2.	
3.	
4.	
5.	
6.	
7.	
8.	
9.	
10.	

Goal Commitment Start Date: ————————————

My life will be different once I complete this goal because (Tell what you see and how you feel):

————————————————————————————

————————————————————————————

GOAL SETTING WORKSHEET

GOAL:
TARGET DATE:
WHY?

KEY ACTION STEP:	DUE DATE:
1.	
2.	
3.	
4.	
5.	
6.	
7.	
8.	
9.	
10.	

Goal Commitment Start Date: ⎯⎯⎯⎯⎯⎯⎯⎯⎯⎯

My life will be different once I complete this goal because (Tell what you see and how you feel):

⎯⎯⎯⎯⎯⎯⎯⎯⎯⎯⎯⎯⎯⎯⎯⎯⎯⎯⎯⎯⎯⎯⎯⎯⎯⎯⎯⎯⎯

⎯⎯⎯⎯⎯⎯⎯⎯⎯⎯⎯⎯⎯⎯⎯⎯⎯⎯⎯⎯⎯⎯⎯⎯⎯⎯⎯⎯⎯

GOAL SETTING WORKSHEET

GOAL:
TARGET DATE:
WHY?

KEY ACTION STEP:	DUE DATE:
1.	
2.	
3.	
4.	
5.	
6.	
7.	
8.	
9.	
10.	

Goal Commitment Start Date: —————————————

My life will be different once I complete this goal because (Tell what you see and how you feel):

_____

_____

GOAL SETTING WORKSHEET

GOAL:
TARGET DATE:
WHY?

KEY ACTION STEP:	DUE DATE:
1.	
2.	
3.	
4.	
5.	
6.	
7.	
8.	
9.	
10.	

Goal Commitment Start Date: ————————————

My life will be different once I complete this goal because (Tell what you see and how you feel):

_____

_____

GOAL SETTING WORKSHEET

GOAL:	
TARGET DATE:	
WHY?	

KEY ACTION STEPS: DUE DATE:

KEY ACTION STEPS:	DUE DATE:
1.	
2.	
3.	
4.	
5.	
6.	
7.	
8.	
9.	
10.	

Goal Commitment Start Date: _____

My life will be different once I complete this goal because (Tell what you see and how you feel):

_____

_____

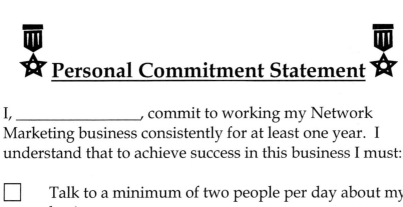

⭐ **Personal Commitment Statement** ⭐

I, _____, commit to working my Network Marketing business consistently for at least one year. I understand that to achieve success in this business I must:

☐   Talk to a minimum of two people per day about my business.

☐   Attend all major Corporate- and Team-sponsored events.

☐   Meet all required sales and recruiting activity each and every month.

☐   Commit to training and personal development.

☐   Find someone to be accountable to: an Accountability Buddy.

I promise to do all of the above listed activities with absolutely NO EXCUSES. I realize that successful people will do what unsuccessful people won't.

_____

Signature

_____

Date

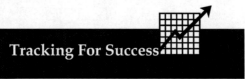

Tracking For Success

Tracking and Accountability is Key. Track results each week no matter what and give your results to your Accountability Buddy with NO EXCUSES. Even a blank sheet tells a story, doesn't it?

Week ____ /Day 1 - Date:_____

Sampled or Piqued Interest

Name:	Date:	Result/Contact Info.:
1.		
2.		
3.		
4.		
5.		

On Sizzle Call

Name:	Date:	Result/Contact Info.:
1.		
2.		
3.		
4.		
5.		

# of 3-way Calls_____ Results:_____

_____

_____

_____

PERSONAL SALES: [   ]   # NEW BOOKINGS_____

TEAM SALES: [   ]   # PARTIES HELD_____

NEW TEAM MEMBERS:_____   # IN-HOME MTGS_____

NEW ACTIVE TEAM MEMBERS:_____   # PRESENTATIONS_____

Training/Personal Development Activity:_____

How do you feel about your progress today?_____

Tracking For Success

Tracking and Accountability is Key. Track results each week no matter what and give your results to your Accountability Buddy with NO EXCUSES. Even a blank sheet tells a story, doesn't it?

Week ____ /Day 2 - Date:_____

Sampled or Piqued Interest

Name:	Date:	Result/Contact Info.:
1.		
2.		
3.		
4.		
5.		

On Sizzle Call

Name:	Date:	Result/Contact Info.:
1.		
2.		
3.		
4.		
5.		

# of 3-way Calls_____ Results:_____

_____

_____

_____

PERSONAL SALES: [   ]   # NEW BOOKINGS_____

TEAM SALES: [   ]   # PARTIES HELD_____

NEW TEAM MEMBERS:_____   # IN-HOME MTGS_____

NEW ACTIVE TEAM MEMBERS:_____   # PRESENTATIONS_____

Training/Personal Development Activity:_____

How do you feel about your progress today?_____

Tracking For Success

Tracking and Accountability is Key. Track results each week no matter what and give your results to your Accountability Buddy with NO EXCUSES. Even a blank sheet tells a story, doesn't it?

Week ___ /Day 3 - Date:_____

Sampled or Piqued Interest

Name:	Date:	Result/Contact Info.:
1.		
2.		
3.		
4.		
5.		

On Sizzle Call

Name:	Date:	Result/Contact Info.:
1.		
2.		
3.		
4.		
5.		

# of 3-way Calls_____ Results:_____

_____

_____

PERSONAL SALES: [   ]   # NEW BOOKINGS_____

TEAM SALES: [   ]   # PARTIES HELD_____

NEW TEAM MEMBERS:_____   # IN-HOME MTGS_____

NEW ACTIVE TEAM MEMBERS:____   # PRESENTATIONS____

Training/Personal Development Activity:_____

How do you feel about your progress today?_____

Tracking For Success

Tracking and Accountability is Key. Track results each week no matter what and give your results to your Accountability Buddy with NO EXCUSES. Even a blank sheet tells a story, doesn't it?

Week ___ /Day 4 - Date:_____

Sampled or Piqued Interest

Name:	Date:	Result/Contact Info.:
1.		
2.		
3.		
4.		
5.		

On Sizzle Call

Name:	Date:	Result/Contact Info.:
1.		
2.		
3.		
4.		
5.		

# of 3-way Calls_____ Results:_____

_____

_____

_____

PERSONAL SALES: [ ]   # NEW BOOKINGS_____

TEAM SALES: [ ]   # PARTIES HELD_____

NEW TEAM MEMBERS:_____   # IN-HOME MTGS_____

NEW ACTIVE TEAM MEMBERS:____ # PRESENTATIONS____

Training/Personal Development Activity:_____

How do you feel about your progress today?_____

_____

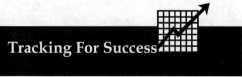

Tracking For Success

Tracking and Accountability is Key. Track results each week no matter what and give your results to your Accountability Buddy with NO EXCUSES. Even a blank sheet tells a story, doesn't it?

Week ___ /Day 5 - Date:_____

Sampled or Piqued Interest

Name:	Date:	Result/Contact Info.:
1.		
2.		
3.		
4.		
5.		

On Sizzle Call

Name:	Date:	Result/Contact Info.:
1.		
2.		
3.		
4.		
5.		

# of 3-way Calls_____ Results:_____

_____

_____

PERSONAL SALES: [   ]   # NEW BOOKINGS_____

TEAM SALES: [   ]   # PARTIES HELD_____

NEW TEAM MEMBERS:_____   # IN-HOME MTGS_____

NEW ACTIVE TEAM MEMBERS:_____   # PRESENTATIONS_____

Training/Personal Development Activity:_____

How do you feel about your progress today?_____

Tracking For Success

Tracking and Accountability is Key. Track results each week no matter what and give your results to your Accountability Buddy with NO EXCUSES. Even a blank sheet tells a story, doesn't it?

Week ____ /Day 6 - Date:_____

Sampled or Piqued Interest

Name:	Date:	Result/Contact Info.:
1.		
2.		
3.		
4.		
5.		

On Sizzle Call

Name:	Date:	Result/Contact Info.:
1.		
2.		
3.		
4.		
5.		

# of 3-way Calls_____ Results:_____

_____

_____

_____

PERSONAL SALES: [   ]   # NEW BOOKINGS_____

TEAM SALES: [   ]   # PARTIES HELD_____

NEW TEAM MEMBERS:_____   # IN-HOME MTGS_____

NEW ACTIVE TEAM MEMBERS:_____   # PRESENTATIONS_____

Training/Personal Development Activity:_____

How do you feel about your progress today?_____

Tracking For Success

Tracking and Accountability is Key. Track results each week no matter what and give your results to your Accountability Buddy with NO EXCUSES. Even a blank sheet tells a story, doesn't it?

Week ____ /Day 7 - Date:_____

Sampled or Piqued Interest

Name:	Date:	Result/Contact Info.:
1.		
2.		
3.		
4.		
5.		

On Sizzle Call

Name:	Date:	Result/Contact Info.:
1.		
2.		
3.		
4.		
5.		

# of 3-way Calls_____ Results:_____

_____

_____

_____

PERSONAL SALES: [   ]   # NEW BOOKINGS_____

TEAM SALES: [   ]   # PARTIES HELD_____

NEW TEAM MEMBERS:_____   # IN-HOME MTGS_____

NEW ACTIVE TEAM MEMBERS:____   # PRESENTATIONS____

Training/Personal Development Activity:_____

How do you feel about your progress today?_____

Tracking For Promotion

First Quarter - Month:_____ Year:_____

# of Team Leaders/A-Players: (Consistent, Available, Active, Accountable)

Name:	Top Producer?	In Separate Leg?
1.		
2.		
3.		
4.		
5.		
6.		
7.		
8.		
9.		
10.		

Assessment of MONTHLY TEAM SALES: (Are they going up or down?):

January	February	March	April	May	June

July	August	September	October	November	December

Date of Next Major Training Event:_____
No. of Leaders Attending:_____ Total Team Members Attending:_____

Name:	No. of Leaders' Team Members
1.	
2.	
3.	
4.	
5.	
6.	
7.	
8.	

Total Team Promotions to Leadership Level:_____

Assessment of Your Leadership Team:_____

_____

_____

Tracking For Promotion

Second Quarter - Month:_____ Year:_____

# of Team Leaders/A-Players: (Consistent, Available, Active, Accountable)

Name:	Top Producer?	In Separate Leg?
1.		
2.		
3.		
4.		
5.		
6.		
7.		
8.		
9.		
10.		

Assessment of MONTHLY TEAM SALES: (Are they going up or down?):

January	February	March	April	May	June

July	August	September	October	November	December

Date of Next Major Training Event:_____
No. of Leaders Attending:_____ Total Team Members Attending:_____

Name:	No. of Leaders' Team Members _
1.	
2.	
3.	
4.	
5.	
6.	
7.	
8.	

Total Team Promotions to Leadership Level:_____

Assessment of Your Leadership Team:_____

_____

_____

Tracking For Promotion

Third Quarter - Month:_____ Year:_____

# of Team Leaders/A-Players: (Consistent, Available, Active, Accountable)

Name:	Top Producer?	In Separate Leg?
1.		
2.		
3.		
4.		
5.		
6.		
7.		
8.		
9.		
10.		

Assessment of MONTHLY TEAM SALES: (Are they going up or down?):

January	February	March	April	May	June

July	August	September	October	November	December

Date of Next Major Training Event:_____
No. of Leaders Attending:_____   Total Team Members Attending:_____

Name:	No. of Leaders' Team Members _
1.	
2.	
3.	
4.	
5.	
6.	
7.	
8.	

Total Team Promotions to Leadership Level:_____

Assessment of Your Leadership Team:_____

_____

_____

Tracking For Promotion

Fourth Quarter - Month:_____ Year:_____

# of Team Leaders/A-Players: **(Consistent, Available, Active, Accountable)**

Name:	Top Producer?	In Separate Leg?
1.		
2.		
3.		
4.		
5.		
6.		
7.		
8.		
9.		
10.		

Assessment of MONTHLY TEAM SALES: (Are they going up or down?):

January	February	March	April	May	June

July	August	September	October	November	December

Date of Next Major Training Event:_____
No. of Leaders Attending:_____ Total Team Members Attending:_____

Name:	No. of Leaders' Team Members
1.	
2.	
3.	
4.	
5.	
6.	
7.	
8.	

Total Team Promotions to Leadership Level:_____

Assessment of Your Leadership Team:_____
_____
_____

Sales Reporting
(Input Sales on Chart and Graph Trends)

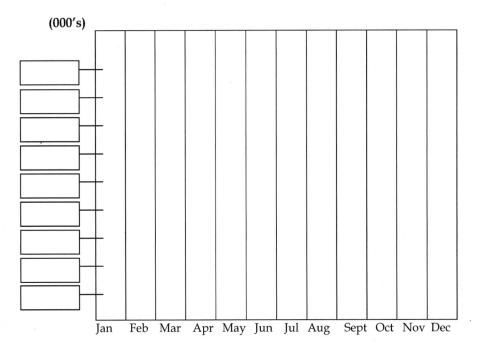

(000's)

Jan   Feb   Mar   Apr   May   Jun   Jul   Aug   Sept   Oct   Nov   Dec

It is important to understand that you are operating a real business and as a business owner, understanding and tracking your sales is key to making a Quantum Leap. In this exercise you are to take your sales for the year and plot them on this graph. January may be your lowest sales month, but if it isn't, you want to put your lowest unit sales in the bottom box on the left side and continue to plot the sales using increments of $5,000 or $10,000 or more depending on the size of your organization and the type of production you have. Once you have a full year of data draw a line from month to month to see the business trends.

Graphs and charts provide pictures for you to get a visual for what's going on with your business. This is a key tool used by most businessmen and women and as an entrepreneur in network marketing, you should use the same tools.

Discuss these trends and your sales with your sponsor and develop plans and strategies to promote healthy growth in your business.

Marketing Promotions

Learning to create awesome team promotions will also assist you in making a Quantum Leap in your business. It is not good enough for you to simply rely on any promotions given by your company. It is always good business practice to create your own team promotions. These promotions help the bonding experience for your team, and also help to foster a fun and competitive, yet friendly, team environment.

You must, however, be careful with promotions. Make sure that you aren't offering more than you can afford to pay out. It always makes good sense not to offer a promotion that is more than 10% of your commission check. Some promotions that work might include:

1. One-prize promotions that call for a drawing and give team members the opportunity to earn entries.
2. Promotions that are offered to the top salesperson and/or top recruiters.
3. Promotions that can earn pins, which can be cost effective.
4. Sell-A-Thons work as well in which you can reward top performers.
5. Recruit-A-Thons work the same way.

Always make sure that the promotions drive the behavior you are seeking from your team. If you want to develop high sales volume, your promotions must be volume-driven. These are always fun. And you never want to run a promotion in vain. You should track the sales volume for the period in which you are running the promotion. What you're looking for is any increases that were a result of the promotion. One-day sell-a-thons can give you sales peaks that are highly visible. With other types of promotions, run over a period of a month, you may want to measure the sales month to month to see if there were any increases in volume. This will enable you to measure the success or failure of the promotion.

Tracking Team Marketing Promotions

Month	Promotion	Results
January		Sales Increase: Comments:
February		Sales Increase: Comments:
March		Sales Increase: Comments:
April		Sales Increase: Comments:
May		Sales Increase: Comments:
June		Sales Increase: Comments:
July		Sales Increase: Comments:
August		Sales Increase: Comments:
September		Sales Increase: Comments:
October		Sales Increase: Comments:
November		Sales Increase: Comments:
December		Sales Increase: Comments:

Life Lesson

The Past Doesn't Equal the Future

Past experiences play through our minds like broken records.
Singing that same old song, telling us what we can or cannot do.
Holding us captive, keeping us trapped in a state that cannot be changed, a place that's gone and doesn't even exist.
Once we learn that the past doesn't equal the future, we unlock the doors of possibility.

We set ourselves Free.

Toni Coleman Brown

Closing Remarks

It's a game. You hear this all the time. Network marketing is a game. You will often hear people say it's a numbers game. But what does that mean? Being told that your business is a game means you should have fun, and play! Network marketing is a simple business that we tend to complicate. Look at it from the standpoint of if you make X number of calls you will get Y responses, and if you attempt to recruit X number of people Y will sign on. These are stats and your stats will change over time as you get better at mastering the fundamentals of this business. That's the numbers game that everyone talks about.

Right now you want to get in the game, but before you get in the game or make a Quantum Leap in your business, you have to leave the locker room. The locker room is that place in most people's minds where they're carrying all of that junk preventing them from going to the next level. It never ceases to amaze me the number of locks people put on their lockers. They have so many combinations of "issues," that they can't begin to find the code to unlock the doors that lead to freedom.

The past is a place that needs to rest in peace (RIP). For most of us, the past represents the point of reference for all future and current decisions. It doesn't matter how big or how small the question is, the answer lies somewhere in the past. Okay, now let's let that marinate in your brain for a minute, while I give you an example to help make it clear.

We wake up in the morning and think about what we want to eat and then we think, "What did I eat yesterday?" And sometimes we say, "Since I had that (toast or cereal or whatever) yesterday and it was good, I'll have it again today." And others may think, " I tried making pancakes and I burned them and set off the fire alarm, so I don't want that to happen today, so I'll have cereal." Whatever you decide, it was based on the past. You go to your closet and you choose what to wear, and you say, "Well, I can't wear that dress today because I wore it yesterday and the last time I wore this suit, it made me look fat and I don't want that to happen again, so I'll wear something different." All those decisions are based on the past. The past is the point of reference for everything. Even in relationships, we tend to be attracted to the same person over and over again and we end up in the same love situations as before because we keep saying yes to that same person who was wrong for us. And that is the problem.

To make a Quantum Leap in your business, you have to understand that your past does not equal the future. People have heard this time and time again, but they continue to make their decisions based on past results and as a result, they stay bonded in the locker room. Stop being a prisoner of your mind. Stop making excuses. Release the past and unlock the doors that will allow you to freely step on the court and get into the game.

Remember how the air is up there with Michael Jordan. He is someone who certainly knows what it means to fly above the clouds, and so do I. I can remember the day clearly. I was flying back from New Orleans to New Jersey. For the entire flight we flew above the clouds. The sun was shining bright, so bright, I had to pull down the shade of my window seat. As we began our descent into Newark Airport, we slowly sank down into the clouds and then finally we were underneath them and I could see the airport and the ground below. Everything was covered with snow and the sky was gray. I was amazed. I thought to myself, "Isn't it funny that the sun is still shining bright above the clouds?"

Now, every time it's raining or snowy outside, I always remember that the sun is still shining and I smile. When people ask me questions or make comments like, "Oh the weather is so bad", or when I watch people and notice how they let the weather determine their mood, I just remember the sun.

Don't let the weather determine your attitude. *Live your life as if you're flying above the clouds and remember that the sun is always shining*, because It Is! Always let your light shine in everything that you do!

When it's your time to Quantum Leap, you will. You will become the Michael Jordan of your company. Everything you say and everything you do will reflect your attitude of being in the zone. You will intimidate some people and that's good. If they're afraid, they should be because you're coming with your best game and the best stats ever. Your closing ratio has gone up and your ability to recruit has gone through the roof. You know it's your time to fly and you do it. Live in the thoughts of where you're going and before you know it, you will have arrived. Live! Live! Live! And Fly! Be More....SOAR! Remember it's a game – have fun and play.

Advice from Business Leaders

Contributors

Barbara Page, Executive, Warm Spirit

Tracey Hughes, President and CEO, The Rum Cake Fairy

C. Thomas Gambrell, President and CEO, GBL Seminars

Niambi Jarvis, CEO and Author, Hiyaah Power

Alivn Day, Speaker, Trainer and Sr. Group Vice President of Mountain Movers, LLC

Bonus Essay #1

Network Marketing Is Like a Love Affair

You know how the story goes. You meet the perfect man. It's the beginning of a beautiful courtship. He say's all the right things that you want to hear. You are in awe. He introduces you to all of his friends and family. You can only image all of the wonderful things that are going to come out of this relationship. Your eyes are focused on visions of a great future. There are no flaws in the dreams that you dream.

You felt the same way when you first started your network marketing business. You had visions and dreams of success. You told all your friends, family, neighbors and co-workers about your great discovery. You had finally found your perfect business and nothing could have been better.

Suddenly, as time went by, you noticed some changes in your relationship. He stopped calling as much as before. He stopped coming by like he used too. You found yourself putting a lot of effort into a one-way relationship. And you noticed that your business was the same way. You called a customer and they didn't return your call. You reached out to team members and they did not reach back. They stopped attending meetings and you found yourself putting in all the effort to keep things going.

So now both relationships become a little estranged. Doubt, confusion, and frustration start to settle in. You're convinced neither are win-win situations. Maybe you made a mistake. Maybe it's not worth the aggravation. Maybe you should end both relationships.

Deep down inside, you question yourself with "What Ifs." You find yourself lying in bed in the stillness of the night with your mind racing and your heart pounding. You think to yourself that maybe there's something there to salvage.

You regain strength and decide to rebuild the relationships that have meant so much, despite all of the challenges and doubts. You still have the desire, passion, commitment and dreams that once excited you in the early stages.

When it comes to your network marketing business, you should follow those thoughts and Recommit yourself to that passion and love again for your business. Those who stick to it during the tough times are sure to achieve success.

It is important to know that just like any relationship, in your business there will be good times and bad times. You must be able to weather the storms. Be still if you have too. Always connect to the positive and forget the negative. When you want something or someone, nothing will stop you. When it comes to your business, allow yourself to fall in love all over again.

Barbara Page
Warm Spirit Executive
Plainfield, NJ

Bonus Essay#2

Listen To Your Cake

In one short year, I learned the lesson of a lifetime, "Listen to the cake." Like so many others who worked in Corporate America, I felt overworked and under appreciated.

I had fallen victim to sacrificing my dreams and passions to the everyday corporate grind. Unbeknownst to me, my life as I knew it would be forever changed by the whisper of a rum cake.

I first met the cake 12 years ago at my friend's New Year's Eve party. Its moist texture and delicate flavor made my taste buds dance. It was love at first bite. So, I did what any person in love would do; I begged and pleaded for the recipe. My friend couldn't remember the recipe or its origin. Devastated but not discouraged, I scoured cookbooks and tested recipes until I was re-united with my first dessert love.

After sharing the cake with friends, family and co-workers, I was immediately approached with holiday and special occasion orders. My hobby soon turned into a lucrative holiday hustle. In fact, the cake saved me one Christmas by providing much-needed cab fare to the airport when my bank account was, surprisingly and embarrassingly, on empty. As orders increased, the cake's voice grew louder. The thought of traveling uncharted entrepreneurial territory terrified me. So, I took the easy way out, and remained in Corporate America for another eight years.

In 2002, I tested the entrepreneurial waters in network marketing as a Warm Spirit consultant, honing my marketing, customer service and sales skills in direct marketing. The more my Warm Spirit business grew, the more confident I became about being an entrepreneur.

However, the cake continued to whisper in my ear, begging me not to forget our love. Three years later, it threw me a hardball. My 9 ½ year career at Colgate Palmolive ended in a layoff. I was in shock and uncertain of my next step. Friends at Smith Barney, Citigroup and Deustche Bank urged me to return to baking and supply holiday gifts for their clients.

My life-changing "AHA" moment occurred when my cake was given to a top magazine editor, who immediately fell in love with it. That was the moment I connected with my life's purpose and seized my opportunity. My cakes allow me to fulfill my personal passion, bringing others happiness while making my own mark in the business world.

In less than six weeks, the Rum Cake Fairy Dessert Company LLC was established, incorporated and open for business. I was a one-person shop wearing all hats: baker, accountant, marketer, sales person, customer service rep, procurement, inventory and operations manager, shipper and sole investor. My living room quickly converted into a bakery with separate glazing and finishing stations. My bookshelf became a makeshift cake storage unit. Cake boxes, shipping boxes and packing peanuts were stacked to the ceiling. In two weeks time, 75 cakes were baked, packaged, shipped and personally delivered in time for Christmas.

Today, the cake is in commercial production at a contract bakery and national packaging facility. It's a popular dessert at Philadelphia's Bluezettes' restaurant and a New York company cafeteria. My website, www.rumcakefairy.com, is receiving rave reviews. The cake is currently "starring" in a national media campaign. These results would not be possible if it weren't for five key steps to success that served as the stepping stones to my business' immediate success. Your moment awaits you as well. You must be willing to listen for your cake and heed its call.

1) **Listen to <u>YOUR</u> Cake**
That little voice whispering to you in your sleep is your personal "cake call." It's ready to lead you to your business passion and success. Fight the fear and seize the opportunity to create your destiny.

2) **Be in the KNOW**
Read, study, learn all you can about your industry, customers and competition to drive business development, growth and success. Contact the Small Business Association (www.sba.org) or Counselors to America's Small Businesses (www.score.org) for training classes, mentoring, and business plan writing assistance.

3) **Power is in the PEOPLE**
Attend networking events that cater to your clientele. Share your business, service and products. Follow up with contacts. Building your

network will increase your business' word of mouth and referral opportunities.

4)   **Stretching the $$$'s**
"Start ups" are forced to grow on shoestring budgets.   A few of my favorite "dollar stretching" tips include shopping for food staples at discount stores like Target, Wal-Mart and Costco. Check out bestsellers, business resources and current DVDs from the library.   Re-sell unused or gently used clothing to consignment stores or via eBay.   Remember to redeem frequent flyer miles and credit card points for free travel and gift certificates.

5)   **Love Yourself**
Replenish your spirit and energy with a little "ME" time. Meditate. Take a short walk. Enjoy a cup of coffee or tea with a friend. Slip out of the office for a few minutes to enjoy the sunshine.

Always remember that "Your Cake Is Calling...Are You Listening?"

Tracey D. Hughes
President & CEO
The Rum Cake Fairy Dessert Co. LLC
www.rumcakefairy.com

Bonus Essay #3

True Understanding of Time

Whether you are a student, employee, community leader, business owner, or busy Christian, one thing we often share are erroneous beliefs about the concept of time. We attempt to manage our lives upon the foundation of these beliefs and that is where our troubles begin. It is said that belief dictates the scope of our thoughts. It is also said that thoughts lead to the actions we take and those actions repeated over time create our habits. Following the logic above, it is easy to conclude that if your beliefs about time are in error then so are your thoughts, actions and habits as it relates to managing the moments that make up your time.

What is Time?

During my tele-classes, seminars, and productivity coaching sessions, I always ask the question, "What is time?" Without fail, the question is followed by a pronounced period of silence. As I explore the answer to this question with event participants and clients, most concede that they do not know. I often hear, "I have never thought about it before." I ask you. Is it possible to manage something that you have no knowledge or understanding of? There it is. The "AHA" moment.

Funk & Wagnalls New Practical Standard Dictionary of the English Language list 22 definitions for the word time. For our purposes, the most accurate answer I have heard in response to our foundation question above came from one of our tele-class participants. He stated simply, "time is a mental construct. It exists in your mind." I could not agree more. Time as a tangible thing is an illusion. When we speak of time, most people think of a watch or clock. When you ask someone, "What time is it?" not only are there 24 correct answers, but by the time they answer your question fully it is no longer that time. Therefore time is not only intangible, it is also relative and transient.

We have all heard the cliché "Time flies when you are having fun" and most of us have experienced engaging in an activity we enjoy a great deal and have time pass quickly. On the other hand, we have also experienced the feeling of time moving slowly when we are engaged in an activity that we do not particularly enjoy or when we are awaiting an eagerly anticipated event.

Most of us agree that the components of measured time are the future, the present, and the past. The future is time anticipated. The present is current time. The past is time gone by. When we examine the tri-fold nature of time, it is easy to see how fleeting it is. The moments of our future, present, and past flow by rapidly in a continuous stream. You anticipate reading the next word on the page, a part of your future; BAM, there it is in the focus of your eyes, a part of your present, BAM, now it has been read, and it's now part of your past.

Where does your future and past exist?

Your past is stored in your memory and your future exists in your imagination. Both your memory and imagination exist in the confines of your mind. Therefore, your past and future exist in your mind. This is why time is considered a mental construct. Time management is not the true challenge we face. The true challenge is the management of our thoughts about time. You can make what you will of your past. Every failure or horror has a seed of success and blessing embedded in it. It all depends on your perspective and point of view. It has been said that we have 60,000 thoughts per day and 50,000 of them are thoughts we had yesterday. Thus we live our future based on our past as opposed to the limitless possibilities that lie before us. Our pre-occupation with past and fret over the future cause us to allow our present to slip by us unattended, and we allow the moments of our life to be wasted.

Moment management is a more accurate term for what you desire. There is an art to splitting your past from your future and developing the ability to be present in the moment versus thinking about what you should have done or what you have to do. There is an art to splitting your time between your roles, priorities, and goals. It is an art because it is different for each of us and significance is in the mind of the beholder. Split your past from your future and live in the moment. Be present. You cannot manage time - only your thoughts about the events and moments of your life.

From "The Art of Splitting Time Primer: 8 Master Keys for Time Management"

By C. Thomas Gambrell
President and CEO of GBL Seminars
www.gblseminars.com
www.cthomascoaching.com
www.blackbusinessleaders.com

Bonus Essay #4

Leverage Your Network

Networking today seems to be shrouded in mystery and process. It actually is as natural for human beings as breathing air. Being social creatures by nature, we have been created with the ability to share thoughts and ideas that can be utilized by society as a whole...for its ultimate advancement. Networking is one of the means used to increase the collective knowledge of the human race.

Traditionally, network marketers have been taught to make lists of all of the people they know — their neighbors, co-workers, relatives, former classmates, and the list goes on. Today, with the power of technology, we have been afforded the opportunity to expand our networks far beyond what was ever imaginable. The first step — take the limits off your concept of how far your reach can grow. I have found that by visualizing my end result first, I could then begin to create or utilize the network needed to achieve those goals. I will demonstrate how this works in a few examples below.

Networking is a strategic use of the people, institutions and thoughts that come before you. All information is intertwined in one fashion or another. Networking just provides you with the means of uncovering much needed information and resources to move to the next level. When I set out to create Hiyaah Power, I knew I already possessed the information necessary to create a global network of dynamic women. The challenge was going to be figuring out how to connect the dots. By visualizing a network that spanned the globe—before I even began planning the online community—I inadvertently set my mind to using my existing networks to expand into a global one.

First, I started with the traditional method of listing friends, colleagues and acquaintances who might be interested in connecting and networking with other professional women—which would actually increase their networking potential. I let that initial group of approximately 100 women know what the vision was and that I needed their assistance to get there. At that time, they began to reach out to women in their network and tell them about the community I was building. The desire to belong to something bigger than ourselves worked to my advantage. It can work to your advantage as well.

> *As you begin your network marketing career or look to make strategic shifts in your existing vision—take the time to share your vision with key individuals who can assist you in advancing to the next level. There is a level of vulnerability that exists when you open up and share your vision for your business or enterprise with another human being. We deal with fear of rejection, mockery, betrayal or failure. You will find that there will be champions along the way who will expose you to their networks simply because you stepped out on faith to contact them.*

Next, I began to research the organizations, social groups and businesses that were doing what I wanted to do. I knew that if I aligned myself with those established entities in various industries, I would be able to achieve some things that would save me major time, lessen the learning curve and also validate my network. Establishing credibility is key to networking. Knowledge of who's who in your industry demonstrates to those you are looking to do business with that you are serious about your endeavors. Connecting with industry experts and organizations also validates the work that you are doing and puts future individuals and businesses that you intend to network with at ease. It lets them know that networking with you will actually bring value to what they are doing.

> *Take the time to research the industry experts and organizations that can help you expand your network. This information is at your fingertips. First run basic keyword searches on the major search engines or Google. If you have specific questions or don't know exactly where to start, www.AskJeeves.com is a great way to get background information. Next, reach out to the organizations and let them know that you exist. They will most likely let you know of events that they host or others in the industry that you can tap into.*

The third step that I took was to begin getting my events, products and services listed online—where people that I wanted to reach could see them. You do not need a massive marketing budget to gain visibility online. There are online chambers of commerce, faith-based business directories, regional/national professional organizations (e.g. Realtors, CPAs) and more. All of the businesses and the people who head them are potential networking partners.

> *Take a look and see if and where your vision fits into what others are doing. Where you see a fit—make the connection. Reaching out and letting people know that you and your product/service exists is the easiest way to*

grow your network. It may not convert to a sale right on the spot…but it will translate into future sales.

Finally, I got involved in online conversations with my target market, professional women. This can be done with any business as well. It is the soft sell concept at its finest. By participating in list serve discussion threads (Yahoogroups, MSN, etc.) I was able to show my presence and the fact that I was interested in what other women had to say. Through it all, my email signature with my business information crossed the desks of tens of thousands of women. I was increasing my network by creating name recognition. I still have women come up to me at events across the country saying, "Hey, I receive emails from you…you're the CEO of Hiyaah Power, right?" I can't tell you how other women standing around will then jump into the conversation and say, please tell me more about what you do. Perfection. Someone else has created an open door for a membership sale, validated my organization and increased my network all in one fell swoop. You can do the same.

Add your detailed business information in your email signature. You never know how many people will receive your emails – that is what I call leveraging viral communication or marketing.

Leveraging your network to increase your business requires creativity, lack of fear, tenacity and the willingness to reach out to others and let them know what you are doing. Our existing networks are more powerful than we realize; they are goldmines that are often taken for granted. You may unearth your most loyal clientele, strongest strategic partners, and industry champions by tapping into this powerful resource.

Bonus Essay #5

Warning – Success Ahead - Danger at the Peak

Have you achieved a great level of success in the game of network marketing? If so, you may be facing grave danger. If you have not yet attained superb success, but you intend to do so, let this be a warning that will help you avoid one of the most ironic, stealthy sources of danger in the business of success…the enemy of success.

I know a young man, let us call him Giovanni Franklyn, who, within three years of starting his network marketing career, began to experience spectacular outcomes. People treated him like a rock star…almost anything for an autograph, a word, a touch from him. Huge crowds paid and attended sessions where he was to present. Each morning, he was free to wake up *after* he was done sleeping; his $5,500 per month job was far behind him; he was earning upward of $40,000 per month. His address, wardrobe and car keys had all been recently upgraded. How could life get any better? It didn't.

Giovanni was convinced he had found the formula to life, so he decided to *build three tabernacles and inhabit there*…in normal speak, that means, freeze the moment and stay there forever. Lo and behold, the greatest enemy of success sneaked up and bit him incurably. He refused to change – and after all, why should he?

Why should a successful person change? Isn't success the ultimate aim? And *if it ain't broke,* why should he fix it? This is a common strategic error committed by many individuals who get to the proverbial peak of their careers.

Today, the rate of change is so rapid that anyone who refuses to change automatically falls behind. Technology, information, business processes and more – all are changing at a dizzying pace. Avoid the seduction of thinking that the attainment of your greatest dream and grandest desire is an excuse for you to stop, pack up your climbing gear and simply enjoy the place where you have arrived. Even that thing at which you have succeeded itself is changing.

Giovanni refused to adapt to the new ways of presenting; the new language to attract busy people; new computerized ways of tracking his business; and, new approaches to recognize and promote his people. As if those changes were not bad enough to ignore, there was an even more critical change that he refused to experience.

Giovanni *himself* needed to change. He needed to grow. He had encountered rapid success despite certain personality and behavioral flaws he had had from the start. When people disappointed him, he did not hesitate to insult and embarrass them. Mix into the recipe a dash of political maneuvers, egotism and avarice, and the cake you bake is called Giovanni Franklyn. In all the years in that business, his attitudes and thinking never improved. He was doing great and so he never worked on himself.

Staying on top in network marketing or any business for that matter, requires more than keeping up with changing technologies and business practices; that's the easy part. The tough part is to continue changing yourself—to improve, grow and become more mature and mellow in your thinking, attitudes and behavior. Unless this level of ongoing change characterizes your journey, the destination will become elusive and disappointing.

Years ago, Spencer Johnson wrote his book, *Who Moved My Cheese*. It dealt with the need to respond to change. A mouse that became accustomed to finding cheese in a certain place was suddenly bewildered and stumped because the cheese was no longer there. He sought to explain, rationalize and understand the change, but still there was no cheese.

The story is a crafty allegory that shows how we have to be ready to respond to change, or our present place of nourishment will be a future place of starvation.

Let us take Spencer Johnson's notion one step further. Today, it is not enough to respond quickly to change. If you are going to stay ahead, you must be *an agent of change*. It is not enough to respond quickly after the cheese has been moved. If you are going to amass wealth in tomorrow's economy, you must *move your own cheese!*

What am I talking about? Isn't it true that change is disruptive and painful? Yes, that's true. Isn't it true that change creates crises and trouble? Yes, that's true. However, let me tell you one other thing that's also true:

"If you fall asleep in the comfort zone of yesterday's success, you will awake to rottenness and ruin. Times are shifting too quickly. "

Persuasion Power – www.AlvinDay.com

Giovanni Franklyn somehow assumed that the finances, fame, freedom and fringe benefits would always be there, because after working hard for a couple years, he had arrived at the peak. He had succeeded. But success is not a thing or a place. It is a state of being—ongoing, dynamic and changing.

People got tired of dealing with Giovanni's attitudes and began to resent him. Many of his key leaders, including close family members, quit and took much of their downline with them. The management of the network marketing company had heard enough complaints and they responded. They no longer invited him to the podium to speak or gave him public recognition. This poor man was getting no respect.

Furthermore, his income plummeted. A year ago, he couldn't pay his bills and called me to borrow money. I loaned him fifteen hundred dollars and kissed it goodbye. He finally quit the business and joined another network marketing company. The last thing I heard about this man who had reached the peak of success was that he had become a network marketing junkie, simultaneously trying to build downlines in two to three companies.

Now, you may argue that this is an extreme case that does not apply to you. After all, you do not have such bad habits and dysfunctional behaviors. That may be true, but I could tell you a hundred other stories of pretty decent human beings who have refused to upgrade themselves, learn, grow and change. Then the world changed around them. In every such case, the results range anywhere from mediocrity to living below standard, from merely getting by to poverty, from frustration to desperation.

So, a worthy question is, how do you make the changes required to keep you ahead in changing times? You have to step outside the normal and do things outside the mere technical skills and performance requirements needed to keep up in your industry. You don't want to keep up. You want to lead.

Certainly there is a long list of changes you can make to attain and sustain the success you desire...improvements in recruiting and customer acquisition, better product knowledge, organization, communication skills, and so on. However, far beyond the importance of all these tactical and operational changes you can make, there is one need that stands out as the greatest. Ignore it and you will be stuck with only the memories of past successes.

1. READ THINGS WORTH WRITING

The biggest need is to discover and ingest the wealth of personal empowerment; self-help literature that is not taught in schools.

Please tell me why it is, that nowhere in the curriculum of a college, or the syllabus of a high school, do you find instructions on how to:

- Work well with difficult people;
- Make something from nothing;
- Discover your life purpose;

- Apply the power of vision;
- Succeed by failing often;
- Live in abundance;
- Move mountains;
- Fulfill dreams;
- Win;
- Be.

This body of information is available in books, audio program and personal development workshops and conferences. Develop a hunger to find these sources. Search the Internet. Ask the successful independent, entrepreneurial business people you know where they find personal development material. At all cost, break out of the walls that define your present work.

I am talking about a body of learning that develops your personality, your character, your fiber and your unique strengths. Your career will shoot and grow more by developing yourself than by learning additional sales techniques. If you have not been given to this kind of reading, I encourage you to start immediately.

Go to the book store. Look for the personal development or self-help section. Go to my website at www.AlvinDay.com to get the amazing audio program, *Born to Fly* and read the personal empowerment book, *If Caterpillars Can Fly ~ So Can I*. They will make you soar. Start the process. Somewhere in that journey, you will likely make a very curious discovery.

You will discover that what your customers or prospects choose to buy is not your product or service. They buy you. That realization is rather fearsome, intimidating and at the same time, empowering. What you are selling is you. In a world of intense competition, what distinguishes you in the marketplace is not high-quality product or service. People can get high-quality product or service from a hundred sources. You are the unique ingredient. If *you* represent value, if *you* are a contribution, if *you* make the difference in their business…if all of this is true, then they gladly buy the product or service you offer instead of buying it from some other source.

When you make the discoveries and begin to grow from the inside out, you will likely observe yourself changing in many of the following ways:

- Improved focus and clarity of thinking
- Greater acceptance of others
- Higher levels of motivation
- Increased self confidence
- Greater peace of mind
- Lower stress levels
- Less fear of people
- Emotional control
- Fun in your work
- Higher income

When these attributes begin to work together, you will see remarkable effects in your sales results. Better yet, you will experience remarkable improvements in quality of life.

The best way to move your cheese is to move yourself — continually improve *you*. Adapt; be responsive; lead. Even when your cheese is perched at the peak of professional accomplishment, move that cheese before the peak moves. Cling to the peak of yesterday's success and when the peak moves, it will hold dangers of seismic proportion.

Alvin Day
Sr. Group Vice President of Mountain Movers, LLC
www.alvinday.com

About The Author

TONI COLEMAN BROWN
Founder and President of Quantum Leap Productions, LLC
Author, Motivational Speaker and Professional Marketer

Toni Coleman Brown began her professional career as a Financial Analyst with the Port Authority of NY & NJ's Management and Budget Department where she was responsible for a multi-billion-dollar operating and capital budget for some of NYC's most popular facilities like the George Washington Bridge, Holland and Lincoln Tunnels, and The Bus Terminal. Before exiting Corporate America in March 2005, she was as an Assistant Director of Marketing for Black Expressions Book Club, in which she served as one of the original founders of the club and contributing to the growth of the club to over $25 million in sales.

Toni started her first Network Marketing business in the early '90's and fell in love with the industry. After working with a number of different companies, she found her true passion in August 2002 with Warm Spirit. In three short years, she reached the top position in the company and has grown a large business unit, which has resulted in earning a full-time income. In 2005, she made a Quantum Leap in her business and more than tripled her income and is passionate about sharing her experience. Toni trains hundreds of consultants in the industry. She shares selflessly and tirelessly her expertise in the field.

Toni was born in New Orleans, LA. She graduated from Howard University with a Bachelor's in Business Administration majoring in Finance and she also holds a Master's Degree in Creative Writing from City College of New York. Toni and her husband currently reside in Queens, New York, with their two daughters, Sasha and Taylor. She is currently working on writing and publishing her first fiction novel, titled *1000 Kisses*, as she continues to pursue her marketing and speaking career.

Contact info:
Toni Coleman Brown
acole225@aol.com
347-563-7350

Glossary of Key Terms

A-Players – Individuals that are diehard business partners. They can be counted on through thick and thin.

Branding – To create and image that will make you stand out from others.

Business Builders – Individuals that sign on to your business who are interested in building large teams.

Compensation Plan – The chart or table that lays out the requirements for you to get paid in your company.

Downline – A person that you sponsored into your network marketing business and their respective teams.

Google – An online search engine.

Key Words – Key words that are used when searching online.

Legs – Different sponsorship lines within your organization.

Mastermind Group – A group of like-minded individuals that come together to support their goals and cause.

Opportunity Meeting – A meeting that takes place at a specific location and time to present the business opportunity to prospects.

Production – Any sales or recruiting activity that can be measured for a certain period of time.

Prospecting - All activity related to piquing a person's interest into your business to the point in which they're ready to enroll.

Recruiting – The act of enrolling someone into your business. All paperwork is completed and consultant or rep id is assigned.

Search Engine – Computer software used to search data online.

Sizzle Call – A brief call normally three minutes or less used to pique a prospect's interest in the business.

Upline – A person that sponsored you into your network marketing business or anyone above your sponsor in a MLM plan.